STRONG *beauty*

POWER UP THE CHAMPION WITHIN

To Nina,
DREAM so BIG!
Believe strongly in you!
You've got this....
♡ Karen

Strong Beauty: Power Up the Champion Within is a real gem. *It's rare for such an accomplished athlete to share so authentically and openly her success secrets, not just for sports but for life. Filled with practical how-to's, her down-to-earth style makes it easy for others to understand and get started. She provides a unique understanding of the power of emotions, often overlooked in our brain-focused society and certainly overlooked by most athletes, and guides the reader to harness their power. Karen's genuine love for people and her passion to help them succeed comes through loud and clear in Strong Beauty. A must-read for anyone from any walk of life who wants not only to win but to truly succeed in the game of life.*

John White, Director, HeartMath LLC

Karen Furneaux

ISBN: 978-1-7752594-0-4
Karen Furneaux, I Promise Performance, Inc.
46 Eastview Drive, Halifax, Nova Scotia, Canada B3P 1E6
karen@ipromiseperformance.com
www.ipromiseperformance.com

Published in Canada

DEDICATION

My intention with this book is to share with young leaders some success skills designed to help them navigate their own challenges and transitions with a little more ease and preparedness. As an elite athlete, these go-to skills helped me on numerous start lines all over the world, and they now help me prepare for podium performances in my professional speaking career. It took me years to learn—and feel comfortable leaning on—these skills, and I'm highly motivated to share them with others who want to take the fast track to their own success.

I dedicate this book to all the amazing mentors and friends I have in this world. You know who you are! I am fortunate to have people in my life who support me, help me to grow and expand, and continue to help me navigate the waters of life. In particular, this book is for my parents, who have consistently believed in me and encouraged me to strive, and who have always encouraged me to connect deeply with who I am, so I can offer my best to the world in which I live. It is because of them that I have persevered and been granted the opportunity to experience a rich life that is full of grace. Mom and Dad, I am forever grateful for your love, presence and guidance. Csom (pronounced Chum), you have been my mentor and my coach for as long as I can recall. You taught me to believe, and to push my limits to achieve the unknown. I am honoured to have worked with you over the years. You changed my life. Thank you. This book is filled, by the way, with whispers of Promise, my golden retriever, who has been at my side through many challenging times. He is a wonderful buddy and a valued member of my team. To my nieces and nephew, Annie, Mary and Michael, the world holds so much promise for you, but you must work hard. There is no limit to what you can be, do, create or have. I believe in you.

Primarily, though, this book is for all the Strong Beauty souls trying to find their way. I remind you that life is a journey and a game, and with great skillsets and habits, you can overcome any challenge en route to your success. My wish for you is that you find something that truly fires you up and gets you excited about contributing your skills, stories and unique beauty to the world. What you learn about yourself along the way is the real prize!

May each of you mine for the nuggets of pure gold along your own special journey…

With love,

Karen... and Promise

Life

is a

Journey.

CONTENTS

FOREWORD

Karen is an icon in Canadian paddling. She set the bar higher for everyone and became one of the best in the world from the little town of Waverley, NS. She showed how important it is to work hard and chase your big dreams with daily, persistent practice. She showed that strength is all about the size of your spirit and the fight in your heart, and not about your stature, and it will get you to your goals. It does not matter where you come from, small community or large, the spirit to succeed every day is what matters.

Karen modeled that your attitude and approach to your daily pursuits determines your progress and also affects the people around you, contributing to the success of the team. Karen understood this from a young age. She was always willing and committed to doing the work and brought a level of excitement and energy to the practice that was infectious and a pleasure to coach. She did all of this with a smile and with grace, even through some of the toughest times in her life. I think that, in large part because of her, I had one of the happiest and most successful training groups in the whole country, with many national team members.

Best wishes,

Laszlo Latorovszki

You have the power to make a real difference.

INTRODUCTION

The Power of Your "Why?"

For as long as I can remember, I've always been searching for gold. My hometown of Waverley was an old gold mining town in the 1860's. The entrance of those old mines is at the intersection, beside the driveway to my life-long canoe club on Lake Thomas, Cheema. As a young girl, I would spend my time outdoors looking and digging for gold. My mother found a good-sized nugget on our property in Silversides that we used to buy our family piano. That search for gold became an obsession for me throughout my teenaged years on the water and ultimately helped me find, see and appreciate the gold within but I will share those stories later. My first love of sport was gymnastics.

"Karen! Suck your stomach in..." Those words came from one of the gymnastics coaches I had growing up. My form wasn't perfect, and I had to try harder to measure up to the expectations of a demanding observer. "Hmmm," I thought, "how should I breathe?"

I spent far too much of my childhood concerned about not being pretty enough.

I recall being about seven years old and taking swimming lessons at the Dartmouth Sportsplex. One girl there had raven hair. It was beautiful. I stood beside her on the pool deck wishing I had long, beautiful hair like hers. I asked my mom after swimming how that girl's hair could be so shiny and pretty. My mom told me that it was because she ate her vegetables! At the time I hated anything to do with veggies. I found them slimy and gross! I would even pick everything off my pizza except the meat and cheese.

As I became more involved in sports however, I decided that I wanted to become a good, fast swimmer. I came to love vegetables along with their hidden powers, and I started to understand that what I ate affected how I felt in the water. I became far more concerned with being pretty tough, pretty kind, pretty resilient, pretty connected, pretty fast and pretty strong! And I now breathe fully into my belly and let my body be, so I can harness my true power and strength.

My goal is to share this mindset with as many young readers as possible in a bid to support them in their efforts to find their own direction. I started Strong Beauty as a mentorship group for girls that teaches and reinforces qualities such as resilience, self-confidence, respect, appreciation, acceptance, personal leadership and healthy practices. I quickly realized that what was at stake was a much bigger world of possibility. Strong Beauty is the story of my own transition and transformative growth. Strong Beauty is who I am at the core of my being. I've learned—and continue to learn—from many strong mentors throughout my life: my family, friends, partners, coaches, teachers, community leaders, business colleagues and speakers. It's time to pay it forward.

My intention with this book is to share the insights and experiences that have accrued to me through my experiences in a highly successful career in sport and the career transition that followed it. Learning to value and appreciate the beauty within is about more than just medals and muscles. Honing my true strengths and communicating using my unique gifts is a journey that I will continue to embrace. My hope is that you talk about the idea of "the champion within," sharing it with others so we can create a Strong Beauty Tribe around the world. If we can all be more gentle and loving with ourselves, we can help so many more people stand up and be the strong beauty beings that we are, igniting the courage to bring our true grace and light into the world. I am so excited to see us all grow.

Join @StrongBeautyTribe on Instagram!

Download additional resources
at strongbeauty.ca

You can do anything if . . . you put your mind and heart into it.

CHAPTER 1: Motivation is the Goal

"Well at least I'm a national team bitch!" I yelled as I slammed the door and left for practice one afternoon. I was crying as I drove to the canoe club. I felt awful immediately and wished I could take back those words. What did I just say?! Who am I? But she just made me so angry! It was my favorite sweater and my sister, Barb, had lent it to one of her friends...who smoked!

I was sure I wasn't going to get it back and, if I did, it would reek of smoke. The truth was that I was exhausted, and I was scared. I was feeling pulled in every direction. School work, multiple sports, music, friends, family, dramas, future plans. I was trying to please everyone, and it wasn't working. I was failing at Math and English at school and excelling at my sport. I was becoming a nasty person inside and I was bottling everything up. I was nasty to my mother and I was even nastier to my sister. I didn't feel good inside myself. I was heading to a workout that I didn't want to attend. I was done with feeling so much pressure. I felt like I could burst. And I did.

Have you ever bottled up anything for so long it eventually just exploded out of you?

Paddling offered me a retreat from the world. I could just be me. I could do one stroke after the next, spear the water as hard as I liked, and I'd go faster. The more energy and power I put into the water, the calmer my mind became, and the more clearly I could breathe and think. There was something very special and therapeutic about being on the water. It was calming to my teenaged brain. It is still calming to me in any whirlwind emotional storm I encounter.

Emotions and day-to-day dramas are part of who we are, and they give us some pretty interesting clues into what we actually need in order to grow. Learning this lesson is empowering. The biggest awareness lies in being sensitive to the kind of energy we give to the situations we experience. What fuel do we use to feed the fire, and which fire do we choose to stoke?

Make no mistake, I am no master. This is not a preachy "I've-figured-this-all-out" advice book. I work on this every day. My journey through my emotions is ongoing. Learning more about them, and the power of my brain, has helped me become a better version of me. A version of me who can engage other, more positive emotions on the start line—despite feeling fearful—and produce a world record performance! A version of me who can stand tall and breathe with a full, deep breath when I'm about to give a presentation. A version of me who is loving toward her family and friends and no longer pushes people away. A version of me who shows love toward herself. I want to share that strength with you. I want you to know that I've got your back in this.

A key part of it all comes from the practice of being present, and knowing it is totally OK and cool to just be YOU. I want you to feel safe in this process. Know that I've been where you sometimes may find yourself. I've felt insecure, emotional, timid, confused, afraid and overwhelmed.

Performance and Anxiety

"Next up, from the Taiso Gymnastics Club: Karen Furneaux." The announcement over the microphone came from the chief judge. I swallowed hard and felt sick in my belly. I looked around the crowd and felt my heart pounding in my chest. I was a tiny, shy kid. I felt small. My palms were so sweaty the chalk was making little white streaks on them. This was my first competition, ever. I was 10. I was freaking out.

I acknowledged the judges and approached the uneven bars—my favorite apparatus—and just like the hundreds of times I'd practiced in my mind's eye, I started my routine. Everything went just as I had planned until I got to the most difficult part of the routine, a handstand on the bars. As I kicked up to the handstand, I felt solid and strong. And then I farted! It was a huge sound that, in my imagination, at least, reverberated grotesquely off the walls of the gymnasium. I was immediately embarrassed and ashamed, but I finished my routine. As I walked quickly off the mats and over to my coach, Shawn, he simply smiled and said, "Wow! Jet propulsion!" I immediately knew it was OK to be just me, and we laughed. That was my first competitive experience and although it was not the most positive ever, it was definitely satisfying, and I wanted to do more!

Your life is unfolding here and now. I know you want to be a success. Maybe you want to play for your local hockey team or be an Olympic champion, or a famous artist, writer or dancer. Perhaps you want to help build houses to serve those less fortunate. Perhaps you want to carve out an area of ground-breaking research, or be part of a team that creates the coolest new app or a piece of technology that revolutionizes how we do things. And maybe, just maybe, you have no idea what you want to do, and that's good, too! I encourage you to own the moment, and create your dream wherever you are. Whatever your goal, you are meant for greatness.

Getting really good at stuff results from all the little things we do each day, the "power processes" that we employ that will make a BIG difference in taking us from where we are today, with a dream, to making that dream come true. It's about being really present, consistent and persistent.

A writing colleague, Anne Bérubé, wrote a really interesting book called, Be Think Feel Do: A Memoir. I love her approach, as it encourages us to take our focus out of our heads and the busy-ness of our goals and our to-dos, and bring it back into Being. The magic happens when you focus on the Being and the Feeling, instead of the thinking and the doing. It brings to light how we do things, with what intention and energy. I will go into more depth on this approach later in the book. For now, just take a little pause and be with your breath. Simply Be.

Every one of us has a Strong Beauty champion within who is just waiting to be unleashed for greatness. Staying true to your goals and dreams through your intentional awareness, through purposeful practice, and by surrounding yourself with people who believe in you, will lead to great things for you. You are your most important teammate. And what you practice becomes your performance.

Having been an Olympic athlete, I know that sometimes in life the water is smooth like glass, and other times it's full of waves. I encourage you to learn how to put your head down, get strong and clear-focused, and keep driving forward through those waves. The things that you learn in the waves of life will help you to grow and expand as an athlete, artist, student, writer, performer, and caring human being.

It is important to remember that the power to get through any situation or challenge in life resides within YOU. The secret recipe is YOU. It is about being ALL IN. Invested. Engaged. No matter what. Good times and bad, being invested in YOU means that you've got your own back and you approach yourself and others with love and caring.

When you're having a particularly rough day, pay extra attention to how you're speaking and communicating with yourself and others—how you're being. Imagine speaking to yourself with a kind and loving voice, one that your inner child needs to hear. Ask yourself, with kindness, what you need in this moment. This one still trips me up and I still need to work on it. My voice gets critical and harsh on my tough days and I start making judgements that, honestly, just tire me out and wear me down. My challenge is to acknowledge how I'm feeling, take a few moments in stillness, and be aligned with my breath. This has an immediately calming effect on me and I will explain exactly what I do to be in a more positive state of mind and spirit later in this book.

Know now that you have everything that you need within you to take the next steps that are presenting to you, no matter where those next steps may lead. Opportunities and challenges present as you are ready to handle them. Believe it or not, you are ready now. So, what are you waiting for? Dive in!

I wrote this book especially for you, and in it I offer you some perspectives to consider along your journey. There are some quick, easy-to-implement tips that you can stash in your kit bag to have ready at a moment's notice. And I hope that you enjoy them, share them and, if there's value here for you, I invite you to keep re-reading these words.

Each part of this book includes stories, examples and some practical skills and lessons to examine and apply. You are unique, and you will resonate with some stories more than others. I encourage you to try them on and see how they feel for you. And I invite you to consider this as your tool box to performance, packed with ideas and inspiration.

Enjoy! And remember, I'm just this tiny little kid who farted in her first gymnastics competition! If I can do this, you can too!

Create Your Own Story

Do you have a goal? If you do, that's great. If you don't, that's great, too.

I want to share a process with you for starting to feel out some goals or intentions. Here goes: today, you get 86,400 seconds. 86,400 seconds! That's equal to 1440 minutes... This is the time that everyone gets every day. We spend about one-third of that time sleeping, another one-sixth of that time eating and/or preparing food. We spend approximately another one-quarter of that time at school or at work.

If we all have the same amount of time, why are some people more successful than others? I believe that how you choose to energize the time that you are given makes all the difference in life. You can do anything you want to do. This book shows you how you can make the most of your time and learn the skills that will allow you to repeatedly hack into your personal best performance in your sport, in school, in work and in life.

So, I want you to really give some thought around what you really want for you. How do you want to feel? How do you even set a goal? What does success look and feel like for you? What is your WHY? What drives you to improve? I'm not suggesting that you map out your entire life plan. Even if you have an intention around where you want to go, that is enough. What fuels you? What are you most excited about? What things or situations give you energy? What things don't you like to do, and what scares you the most?

Give some thought to these questions and I recommend you write your responses in a journal. It's a good idea to keep revisiting these questions and it is OK if things change for you! These questions are like the layers of an onion: each time you revisit them, you get closer to the core. Consider this journal the sacred space for you to dream, vision, project, and transmit. Think of it as a picture, a moment in time that is captured on paper or online. It represents the framework and the reality that you're currently working with. Each time you go through the process of answering these questions, you will become more clear about your goals and intentions. The world is yours to create. Ready?

Goal Getting

If you have achieved one of your goals by this point, that's great! Give yourself a huge hug to celebrate, and find another goal. If you're not there yet, decide what you want to achieve. This is a big step forward. It helps to chart a path. Goals put energy into the world, and with energy comes intention and practice and, over time, it yields results.

Write It Down

I find transcribing my goals onto paper or into my journal helps me to clearly articulate what I want to achieve. Writing makes it more concrete than just a fragment of thought that may slip away or avoid attention.

Share It

If you feel like it, sharing your goal with someone you trust is even more powerful. That makes it real with some built-in accountability. I Promise, when you tell someone about your goal, they will ask you about it.

Power It Up by Breaking It Down

You add power to your goal when you break it into smaller, meaningful, chunks, stages or steps. This helps further define it, and starts to create a timeframe for achieving it.

Plan It Out

Think of what the first step toward your goal might be. Who do you need to connect with, what should you focus on, and how can you start? The key is to start! Two thousand years ago, the Greek philosopher, Aristotle, said: "Well begun is half done." There is truth to that. Starting a task or a goal requires the most energy. Once you start, you can gather forward momentum and keep things moving. Sir Isaac Newton, a 17th Century physicist, described this phenomenon as well when he said, "An object at rest will remain at rest unless acted upon by an external force." Having a plan helps to gather momentum for movement!

See it, Feel it!

Imagine success. Visualization is no longer considered a hocus pocus thing that people talk about doing. Research has shown that surgeons, pilots, presenters and athletes can use visualization to enhance their performance. The power of the mind is immense, and scientists believe that we may experience real-world and imaginary actions in similar ways by activating the same neural networks. We can train our brains to do, feel, think and see amazing things, and there is plenty of evidence to show that visualization can help patients recovering from brain trauma or stroke as well!

In 2015, my mom had a stroke that affected the right side of her body. Her occupational therapist had her training with mirror boxes to get the use and function of her right arm back. She would practice the movements with her left hand and when she watched them reflected in the mirror, her brain thought that her right hand was moving. It's fascinating how this works! My mom is way too smart to believe that the affected arm was actually doing the movements she was seeing in the mirror, but what was happening was that the illusion helped her brain rewire itself through a process called neuroplasticity. Our brains are plastic and ever-changing, and neuroplasticity allows us to initiate new neural pathways to learn and re-learn tasks. As the brain processes the motion it sees in the mirror, it is re-learning how to send signals to move the body! The mirrored neurons induce the motor neurons to improve motor skills.

Visualization has received some good air time through television broadcasts of athletes' dressing rooms. We can now see an athlete as he or she prepares to take to the ice before a figure skating competition, warming up their minds as much as their physical bodies. At the top of the mountain, we now have eyes into the preparations that alpine ski racer Lindsey Vonn goes through before she tackles the most demanding mountains in the world. We see Kaillie Humphries before she pilots the bobsleigh down the most demanding tracks in the world. Most important to the visualization process is to make it real. Feel it. Put yourself there in the moment in your mind...

Keep Going!

The key to goals is to keep fuelling them by keeping them ignited. Keep working towards your WIN every day. That WIN is What's Important Now. Keep doing that and coming back to that. Momentum is what counts here. Keep the motion going as long as you're still fired up and excited about your goal. Movement always represents progress along the path.

Celebrate the Micro Wins!

A win is a win, is a win! No matter how small it is, start feeling a sense of celebration, experience how it feels to win and accomplish some success with your goals. The win feels good, and it will keep you coming back! You will experience at least one win every day. Sometimes you have to look for it, but I Promise, it's there!

If you still need help in defining your goal, I encourage you to use the S.M.A.R.T.E.R. formula that I sometimes use for my own goals.

S.M.A.R.T.E.R. Goals in Seven Easy Steps:

American philosopher Elbert Hubbard once said: "Many people fail in life, not for lack of ability or brains, or even courage, but simply because they have never organized their energies around a goal." S.M.A.R.T.E.R. goals are an excellent way to organize your energies and here is how they work:

S = Specific, clearly defined

M = Measurable, with a definition of success or completion

A = Agreed upon, where there is agreement among all stakeholders

R = Realistic, and achievable with the available knowledge, resources, etc.

T = Timely, so there is enough, and not too much, time

E = Energized, so they are engaging to pursue

R = Recorded, with trackable success and measures

Here is a template for you to try when setting your S.M.A.R.T.E.R. goals!

Setting S.M.A.R.T.E.R. Goals in Seven Easy Steps

Start by completing this chart:

Name: ______________________________

Date: ______________________________

Goal: ______________________________

Reason this goal is important to me: ______________________________

____

____

Now add in more detail:

SPECIFIC

What is it you want to achieve in your life? Think about what is important to you right now. A good goal statement explains the what, why, who, where and when of a goal. If your goal statement is vague, you will find it hard to achieve because it will be difficult to define success.

MEASURABLE

It is helpful to be able to track progress and measure the result of your goal. A good goal statement answers the question, how much or how many. How will I know when I have achieved my goal?

AGREED

Your goal must be relevant to your stakeholders and secure their agreement. You might include here your coach, your teacher or your manager. Think about your why here, and relate this back to your values and personal mission.

REALISTIC

Your goal should stretch you, but be realistic and relevant to you. Make sure the actions you need to take to achieve your goal are within your control. Is your goal achievable?

TIME-BOUND

Goals are most effective when they have a firm timeline. A good goal statement will answer the question, "When will I achieve my goal?" Without time limits, it's easy to put goals off and leave them to die. As well as a timeline, it's a good idea to set some short-term milestones along the way to help you measure progress.

ENERGIZED

Are you still passionate and excited about your goal? Does it give you positive energy? Ask yourself the question from time to time and remember it is OK to modify your goals if they no longer resonate with you.

RECORDED

Always write down your goal before you start working towards it. Journalling is a valuable practice in this regard. Written goals are visible, and therefore have a greater chance of success. The recording is necessary for the planning, monitoring and reviewing of progress.

To download the Goal Setting in Seven Steps worksheet, please go to: strongbeauty.ca

Connect to What Matters to YOU: Design Your "Dream Board" Collage

I find creating something from my heart is helpful when I feel overwhelmed. It helps me to feel centred, and to find motivation and inspiration.

When I was about 15 years old, I started creating vision boards. These were poster-sized boards filled with inspirational words and pictures that I would paste together to form a collage. I would mount one on my bedroom wall along with some magazine cuttings or articles that inspired me. One of my favourites included a picture of Picabo Street, an American ski racer in the 1990s, and it had featured in a ski magazine beside a quote from her that said: "My grade 12 report card comments were: 'lacks focus and clear direction'. I posted this comment beside a picture of me skiing off a 40-foot cliff!" It served as powerful motivation." Picabo Street went on to win multiple Olympic and world championship medals.

I would post goal times on my wall and I proudly hung my medals there. With each upcoming Olympiad, I'd ask my dad for a flag from the host country. Every morning, I'd wake up and see those flags, as well as all that inspiration, and I'd start my training day from there. This is a practice I still find helpful today. Here is a copy of a vision board that I recently created:

What is your vision? Can you feel it or see it? Use the space below to describe your vision with words and pictures. When you give your vision this energy, I Promise, it starts to expand!

Ready?
Let's
do this!

CHAPTER 2: Honour YOU and Where You've Been

I remember being eight years old and obsessed with the Olympic Games. More than anything, I wanted to be an Olympian. When I played with my friends, we would always end up playing "Olympics." We would do flips and hold gymnastics competitions and sprint races on the lawn. We would be out the door when the sun came up and back only in time for supper, all summer long. I distinctly remember a conversation with my Grade Three teacher, Miss Fehr, about my dream to become an Olympian, and I remember writing stories about my experiences as a gymnast. Miss Fehr always listened to me and encouraged me, and I will never forget that. In fact, today I get to speak to thousands of school-aged kids as part of my role with the Nova Scotia Sport Hall of Fame's Education Program. I always try to listen to the kids, and the stories that they share with me, just like Miss Fehr listened with intention and presence to me.

What do you remember most vividly from your childhood? Think back to some of the stories and experiences that shaped who you are today. Maybe you had to deal with a particular challenge. Think back to the skills and strategies you learned in order to do that. Perhaps you had a significant moment of clear vision or passion, or perhaps that hasn't happened yet. All of that is good stuff! I invite you to pause to reflect on your youth and be grateful that you are YOU. Everything that you have experienced has helped frame who you are now. And who you are now will help guide who you will become. The empowering part in all this is that you choose.

My mom and dad encouraged my sisters and me to be active. I remember learning to swim in Lake Thomas at the Cheema Aquatic Club in my hometown of Waverley, Nova Scotia, and participating in the "Kiddie Kayak" program there. Those days were full of laughter, screeching, and a flurry of water activities. Cheema is a place of summer and sun for me—those bright yellow boats and the smell of fibreglass in the sunshine became deeply-seeded memories that I love to this day. I watched the older kids leaving the dock in their racing boats and I wanted to go with them. Kayaking demands balance and timing, and for one whole summer I was at the dock, learning to stay upright in the boat.

In my mind, Cheema is a little slice of heaven. What I found out years later was that Cheema is a Mi'kmaq word, meaning: "to paddle." I had studied the Mi'kmaq people in school and learned about their trade routes, their boat building and their use of the Shubenacadie Canal and waterway. I imagined being part of this amazing warrior tribe when I was paddling in the war canoe. I thought it was so cool that canoe clubs had formed along these ancient routes.

Waverley had been a gold mining town at the turn of the last century. It was a village right out of the wild west. People came to mine the gold and seek their fortunes from the hills and waters of Waverley. It was fitting that our little canoe club's colours were black and gold, to signify the gold and the dirt that marked our community's past. Over the years, and still today, our Cheema continues to mine so much gold!

I always felt that our little lake was filled with story and greatness. Passion and power, and blood, sweat and tears. So, I paid homage to it and acknowledged our history the best way I knew how: I gave to it my best effort and most positive intentions, pouring every ounce of my strength daily into the water, and feeling grateful to be connected to it all.

I started getting pretty good at kayaking by my second summer and I entered a couple of bantam races—for kids who are in their middle-school years. I recall one race in particular that took place at the Pisiquid Aquatic Club in Windsor, Nova Scotia. I was competing in a full-sized solo racing kayak, a K1, for the first time. It was the tippiest, most difficult boat that Cheema owned, and I could stay upright in it! As I paddled up to the start line and waited for my race, I heard a loud crack. The steering stick between my toes was moving without any resistance. My steering cable had broken! I had no time to fix it or jump into another boat in time for the race, so I just lined up and hoped for the best...I probably paddled double the distance of my competitors that day, with all the weaving back and forth I had to do. I tried with all my might to stay in my lane. I finished the race, and was so proud that I didn't fall in! Sometimes, you just have to muscle it.

I figured out pretty quickly in my kayak life that all success required was that I out-work my training partners. I loved being on the water and going as fast as I could with my own power and strength. I had only one goal for every training session: to go as hard as possible and leave everything on the water. There is nothing like the total, pleasant fatigue that comes from an incredibly tough workout. I knew if I pushed myself hard every day to get faster, I would experience even more beauty in my sport.

A Bumpy Path to Success

I remember the first day I met Csom, my first serious racing coach. He came to Canada from Hungary, and he loved Cheema, our little canoe club. He has a terrific way about him that lets you know that he is a coach and a leader, and I knew he wanted me, and all the other people on the team, to achieve our own greatness. He wanted us to lead our own race. He inspired strength, courage, power and passion, from his little metal coaching boat with only a megaphone for support.

Many foggy mornings saw me trying to find the little hole in the bridge that hid the entrance to the second lake on which we trained. Csom would call encouragement to me above the putt-putt-putting of his motor boat, and the gentle lapping of the water against the side of my kayak gave me a feeling of peace, belonging, and purpose. Like the previous coaches at Cheema, Csom fostered a club of greatness. He inspired a way of being. He expected us all to show up every day and give our best effort. If you did that, you earned his trust and respect. If you let him down, he quietly let you know. We were willing to go the extra miles for Csom.

Csom came to Cheema in the fall of 1991. He could say a few phrases in English like, "Go Beach Near…", which meant paddle close to the shore, for safety and practicality. He had to track about 30 kids who were on the water in boats—no easy task. He would also say: "Change your clotheses," when it was time to change into dry, warm clothes after training.

Csom made every day about fun and competitive spirit and he had a trick to motivate the girls on the team, too. Because we all trained together, we started in one massive group, with the boys behind the girls. The fastest kayakers and canoeists would start behind the slower athletes. The faster you were, the further behind you started, and you had to try and catch the frontrunners and then hold on. It allowed us to have a little race at the end of our training set. I never wanted to be beaten by the boys at the end, and I always found that little extra gear when I felt the boys moving up!

While I attended high school, I was also studying piano. I recall sitting at one of my piano lessons after school and my teacher, Mrs. Lightfoot remarked on my hands. She took them in hers and rubbed the callouses and said to me, "Girls shouldn't have blisters and callouses on their palms." Right away, I knew we were very different women with much different goals. She could teach me piano, but my passion lay with the paddle.

A Surprising Turn of Events

By 1993, I was 17 years old and competing in two different sports. I was a passionate ski racer and a sprint kayaker. But, I was a ski racer at heart...I loved the feeling of speed that screamed through me on the slopes of the Wentworth alpine ski hill in Nova Scotia's Cobequid Hills. I would sharpen and tune my own skis before a big race weekend, and I went as fast as I could through the gates. Back in those days, I'd tape all of the World Cup ski races and, of course, the Olympic games, on our VCR to study and watch after school. I took in each skier's different techniques for success. I was a ski racing fanatic!

By this point I was trying to make the Nova Scotia Canada Games ski team. I wanted the cool jacket and the backpack that team members proudly wore! One evening at Wentworth, I was doing some Giant Slalom (GS) training, and just taking a warm-up run down the Rosebowl trail—one of the easiest trails on the mountain—with my friend, Cara. We were doing huge, fast GS turns, when, suddenly, we crossed each other's path. We collided at top speed. My face hit Cara's knee and we both went down. It took me a few tumbles before I could stop and, after sliding on the hard-packed snow, I thought that I was OK. But when I tried to speak, I inadvertently pushed some teeth out of my mouth. In an instant, I had knocked out my left front teeth, and impacted one of my canine teeth. As I was to find out later, my mouth was a wreck. I was tobogganed down the rest of the hill and an ambulance took me to Truro hospital to undergo emergency dental exams and surgery. My parents met me at the hospital and, at 11:30 p.m., my dad subbed in as the dental surgeon's assistant.

Together, they started the long journey towards putting my face back together… and I am so grateful! I'm not sure to this day if I suffered any concussion, but I was foggy, to say the least, for many days after that. I did not know then that it would take nearly two years to fix my teeth. I had to undergo many painful dental surgeries, bone and skin grafts and dental implants, as well as root canals. My new teeth made me look tough—and I didn't mind! My parents' attitude through all of this was key. It had been an accident. It was not anyone's fault that I was in such a perceptively challenging state. I had been in the wrong place at the wrong time. But maybe I had been in the right place? That ski accident made me decide that I wanted to pursue kayaking full time! As soon as I could, I channelled all my energy into training for kayaking.

In the summer of 1994, on Cheema's 25th anniversary, our little club won the national championships for the first time in many years. This was a huge feat. Just a few short years after Csom's arrival, we rose from insignificant in terms of the overall title to being the best canoe/kayak club in the country! We were the little club that could! We had a fun and awesome group of kids, and everyone contributed to that club win. A week or two after our triumph, right before school started, the newspapers came to take pictures of our team on the village green in Waverley. I had undergone a painful dental operation right after nationals and my face was swollen on one side, but I was so proud and fierce! I was shining and smiling with inner pride and beauty!

And then I started my first year at Dalhousie University. Cheema's club colours were black and gold, Waverley's colours were black and gold, and, likewise, so were Dalhousie's. It was an obvious choice for me! I love black and gold! What's more, the university mascot was The Tiger. I was a really good runner throughout my high school years and I was asked to run at university as well. For a short season, I was a Dalhousie Tiger. My mom gave me a little stuffed tiger when I graduated from high school and I carried it with me to races all over the world.

I never excelled academically at high school, although I always did well at my work. I've always loved learning, and still do today. But university was where I truly excelled. I loved picking my classes and setting up my degree path. I scheduled my classes around my kayak and running training, and I completed my full-time studies at Dalhousie while training and traveling around the world.

On the first day of school though, I met Annette MacLean. We were both lost inside the Dalplex looking for our physical education class. As it turned out, she was the girl with the raven hair who had been in my childhood swimming classes! We actually discovered that we had also competed together in gymnastics many years earlier, as well. My name, Karen, is Annette's middle name, and her mom's name was Allison, which is my middle name. We became fast friends!

That first week of class was a little bit intimidating for me. My face was healing from the dental surgery and it was still a bit swollen. Besides Annette, I didn't know many people, but in my sport history class, I met many athletes from other sports and I immediately felt at home. I made it a habit to introduce myself to my professors and let them know that I'd be traveling at some points of the year with my kayaking schedule. All of the professors in the physical education and kinesiology departments were welcoming to me. Dr. Sandy Young immediately said he knew who I was and had been following my sport career. I felt a sense of family at Dalhousie, and I was introduced to the Nova Scotia Sport Hall of Fame through a free education program at the end of the first term. One of our class assignments was to attend the gala ceremonies at the Sport Hall of Fame and I sat in the audience at the Halifax World Trade and Convention Centre as the name of my first ever kayaking coach, and Cheema's first Olympian kayaker, Ann Dodge, was announced. The founder of the Cheema Aquatic Club, Frank Garner, was also inducted into the Hall of Fame that night! This was a supremely special experience and from that moment on I was interested in volunteering for our Nova Scotia Sport Hall of Fame.

I continued training with Csom while at Dalhousie. He was to be my coach for 17 years altogether, and he was with me through the good times and the bad. We probably spent upwards of six hours a day together, along with the other athletes in my training group. One of the qualities that I loved about Csom as my coach was his ability to connect with each athlete and treat everyone's goals as important. He helped everyone, honouring each of us with his teachings and his time. Because of his boundless belief in me, my belief in myself also grew. Our training sessions were a mix of on-water training, weight room workouts and trail running. I'd play my favourite motivational songs, which included "Back in Black" and "Thunderstruck," by AC/DC, and "Eye of the Tiger," by Survivor. In the winters, Csom would sometimes train with us, skiing and trail running. We were not just simply going through the motions. I learned to push the limits of my physical capabilities. I developed the mental fortitude and the courage to dream, to push and to grow.

I was smaller than my racing colleagues around the world, but I had a strong 5'5", 125 lbs /165 cm, 57Kg frame. My competitors had at least 20 pounds and four inches on me. But I was mighty and filled with fire. I always knew that to compete, I had to out-work the world. And out-work the world, I did! I learned the principles of building a solid training practice and I developed a level of personal grit that just seemed to pull me through when I needed it. But that grit came through learning to welcome the work. Persistent, consistent work. There are no short cuts to doing the work.

Success Moment

"I was competing with a lot of teammates for a spot on the Olympic K4 (four-person kayak) team. I remember thinking to

myself when I woke up that anything could happen that day. Instead of fearing the upcoming seat races, I chose instead to think and, most importantly, FEEL positively about the training that I had done, and I actually started seeing how the races would unfold. I saw only success. There was no other option. If I was going to get one of those coveted spots, I knew that I had to have everything working for me. So, I put my mind and my heart to work for me. I won the seat spot and was named to the Olympic team on that very day. " Karen

Did you know that our heart and our brain are connected?! In fact, our heart sends more neural signals to our brain than our brain sends to our heart. So, focus on feeling positive in times of challenge. You've got this!

Take a moment to pause and recognize your unique value. Remember your favourite moments: summertime at the beach, watching a sunset and all its beautiful colours, hanging with your friends, eating moon mist ice cream after a soccer game, beautiful views. These feelings are your golden moments. They shift your heart from a place of worry, fear or anxiety to a place of presence and connectedness.

When you want to perform in an aspect of life that you are working on, the key is to be connected. Our minds, our hearts and all of our systems in sync. You can tell when you are in this place. It is often referred to as "The Zone." In this place, you feel connected and there is ease. Sometimes it feels as though time passes quickly, as you are completely absorbed in the task at hand. I spent years preparing to compete in the Olympic Games and, as you can see from my story, it wasn't always easy. There were setbacks and difficulties, as well as triumphs and achievements, along the way.

My golden retriever, Promise, came into my life as a puppy and he's grown with me through happy and hard times. He has taught me the importance of fun, relaxing, playfulness, excitement, energy, movement, connection and living in the moment! I named my company after Promise. He taught me to value nature, and my environment, and he taught me that it's OK to show my feelings. We have taken many meditative walks together and along the way I've also learned how to honour myself first, and recognize that every challenge I've faced resulted in a redirect that put me closer to a better outcome. I invite you to honour yourself and your journey, as well. No matter what it is you're trying to accomplish, it's unlikely that you will steer a straight line course to success. That's OK!

So, go ahead. Be brave. What goals or intentions await you? Make your promise to YOU!

Bring forth your greatest light.

CHAPTER 3: "P" is for Power Up the Present

The biggest secret to success that you will ever learn is that you already have all the elements to create success in your life. You just need to awaken them at the right time. You're always getting stronger and you will gain physical strength and power as you grow and learn new physical skills. You will gain emotional strength as you move through life's up and downs and welcome new experiences. You will gain mental strength as you are tested over and over again. You will gain spiritual strength as you overcome challenges and obstacles. But there is no secret sauce. The secret is YOU. You bring yourself to the arena and it becomes a game with only you in it. When you are not there, you cannot play or perform.

Right now, find a mirror, look into it and say to yourself, "It's ME!" You are the secret weapon and I Promise you, when you bring your best self or your A Game to the start lines of life, it is YOU with whom everyone else will be competing. It is only then that you can be a contender. It is important to bring this self not only to event days and presentations, but to every day. And then you'll realize that anything is possible.

So, how do we arrive in the present moment, so that we can stand confidently in our own skin?

Photo by Marion Michele on Unsplash

We get present, connected and centred. I have an acronym for you. The word is P.O.W.E.R.

P = **Present moment awareness—breathe out**

O = **Open to receive and grow—shift your emotions to the more positive feelings**

W = **Wisdom—recognize where you have strength, and recognize all you have learned**

E = **Energy—hold your intention in the moment**

R = **Respond and take Responsibility**

In this section, I introduce you to the POWER process. When I recognize that I am Power, I am empowered. POWER is an acronym you can quickly call upon and easily recall its message to assist you. I developed these power processes over many years of training to be the best I could be at anything I turned my mind to doing. I'd like to share with you what that journey was like.

Success Systems: Creating Power Processes

Developing a power process is actually even more important than setting goals. It is helpful to envision goals regularly and check-in on their level of importance to you to see if you are still passionate about your journey toward them. But the power process and success system that you employ habitually every day is what will carry the goals through to completion.

Habits and daily focused effort are what we rely on to get us to our goals, so it's important to spend time creating the power process that will bring you towards them. The secret to the power process is that it breaks the goal down into what you can do right now… today. If you put your energy here, and do the work set out in the process, the goal gets done—simple! It's amazing how quickly it happens.

For example: as a kayaker whose dream was to compete in the Olympic Games and become the world champion in my field, my power process was my daily practice routine. I only missed it if I were doing another sport for cross training or I was injured or ill. I trusted and believed in my coach and also believed that, with that process, I could become my best.

Deciding to Be My Best: Honouring My Journey

It took me eight years to make it to the Olympic Games. My process started two years before I began university when I sat down with my coach, Csom, in 1992, and chatted with him about my goals. I told him that I wanted to make the Canada Games Team, which were to be held in Kamloops, BC, the next summer. Csom was completely on my side and we started training towards that goal.

It wasn't all roses and I had an important learning experience around that time after a local regatta. My teammates and I had done really well and during some post-race celebrations we got into some mischief. One of my friends knew the location of one of our rival club's boat trailer and, together, we decided that we should take down their club sign. So, in the night, we went to the trailer and disassembled the sign and took it back to our club at Cheema as a prize. I went along with this adventure because I wanted to fit in. I knew deep down that it was wrong. I wanted to be part of the crowd and share in the fun. But the adventure, as it turned out, was not fun. I felt scared that we would be caught. I also felt bad because I pictured some of the dads of the club attaching the sign to their trailer like the dads had proudly done with our club sign at Cheema. I went home that night and told my parents what I'd done. My dad told me that if I wanted to be successful in my life, I'd have to make some choices. Sometimes those choices would have to be around diverging from the group norms and the status quo. Sometimes they would involve a tough decision and sometimes they would be easy. He told me how important it was for me to choose my own path. Those were wise words of wisdom. Our decisions are reflected in our lives every day. We are all nothing more than the sum of all our decisions. The next morning, we had to re-attach the club sign onto the trailer.

In the fall of 1992, I was named to the Canada Games core team as an outside possibility and I was excited. I trained hard that year, throwing myself into weight training, swimming and kayaking on the water as soon as April arrived, and the ice melted. Training started at 6:00 a.m. before school, and then resumed again for the evening right after school. I went to Florida that winter for three weeks for my first spring training camp, missing two weeks of

Grade 12 in the process. That spring, I went to the Canadian trials and became inspired by the beauty of Ottawa. I looked down Mooney's Bay from the start line and saw the gold roof of the St. Elias Antiochian Orthodox Cathedral, and I admired the view of the Rideau Canal from the Rideau River. I remember watching many of the senior national team members doing their starts. I was impressed!

I raced my heart out and earned a place on the Junior World Championship team. I was 16 and no one knew who I was! I headed off to the Czech Republic to represent Canada for the first time at the Junior Worlds. My little goal of making the Canada Games team had turned into something much bigger. I learned then that if I simply set a goal and consistently, persistently practiced and devoted my time and energy to it, I'd achieve something great! It was so worth it! I stroked the K2 and the K4 (for two- and four-person boats respectively) and when I was on the start line at those championships I felt like I was exactly where I needed to be! It was an incredibly special experience, but I very quickly learned how much more work I had to do to be among the best! Wow! I made it my mission to continue to train as fast and as hard as I could to be able to race the K1 at the World Cup the following year. World Cup racing offers a training ground and an opportunity for athletes to test and fine tune their race tactics and techniques for the World Championships or Olympic Games. It's demanding!

Earning the Right to Race

I recall being so proud of my Team Canada uniform, especially my red racing shirt. It was just a simple cotton T-shirt, but that racing shirt transformed me. The Maple Leaf was on the left side of the chest and the word "Canada" was screened on the back. When I pulled that T-shirt over my head I felt like Wonder Woman! I embraced that feeling each time I raced.

The following year, in 1994, I earned the right to race the K1. I went to the Canadian trials and won all of my races. I was even named to the national team and received funding for training and competing for the first time. I was so proud that I received $350 per month from Sport Canada! I thought I could buy a car! I also attracted my very first sponsorship and, from that moment on, I was drawn to the business of sport and the idea of creating my own income and funding.

That summer, I got to train with the very best Junior athletes in Hungary, my coach's home country. The Hungarians are known for their ability to produce top-level kayakers. The opportunity intrigued and inspired me, and the training was intense. We would run up and down the hill at the top of which was perched Castle Visegrad, in Vac, Hungary. We would paddle with the big European cargo movers in the mighty Danube. We would eat apricots and palacsinta, Hungarian pancakes. No wonder these athletes are so good! At the World Cup in the Netherlands that year, I placed second in the world. This was my first international medal and I became completely hooked on competition!

In 1994 I told Csom that I wanted to be the stroke of the national team K4, to hold the lead seat and be the pace setter. I was small and mighty, and I had a lot of spirit and spunk. But our Canadian women's K4 at the time was ranked among the top three teams in the world. It was incredibly "out there" and audacious to aim for the pilot seat of that boat. Csom said to me that if I wanted to do that, he would support me in my efforts, but I'd have to train harder than ever, and become faster than before. His motto: "If you always train at the same speed, you stay at the same speed. It's good for fitness, but not for performance." That message stuck with me and I think there's a little of Csom reflected in the name I chose for my company, I Promise Performance.

I looked up to many of the ladies on the national team and many of them embraced me and mentored me. I identified with Alison Herst the most. She was the stroke of the women's K4 at the time and she was exactly my height, although she was built a little more sturdily than me. The first time I broke the two-minute barrier at nationals was when I was racing at my favorite course, in Ottawa. My time was 1:59.55. After the race, Alison congratulated me and said to me that if she could do it, then I could too! That moment was etched in my mind and for the next 17 years, I became obsessed with my times and my race against the clock. I was becoming a student of my sport and loved strategizing over how to make my time faster!

Breaking Through the Barriers

At our home world championships in 1997, my dream to stroke the women's K4 finally came true on Lake Banook. I wanted to raise the bar for myself and my team, to break through my previous barriers and achieve results far beyond what people expected. We raced to many world cup medals that year and capped the season off with a strong and close fifth-place finish at the Worlds in the 500-metre event. The world cup season is a series of races where athletes can accumulate overall points. It is an opportunity to test and hone racing skills and tactics and this win was magical. We also won a stunning and surprising silver medal at the World Championships in the sprint event, K4 200-metre. My favorite moment of all came when I crossed the finish line of the 200-metre K4 race with my paddle over my head. I felt euphoric in the wake of the final push from my amazing crew mates, and I happened to look over to see the notorious Birgit Fischer, a renowned, in fact an iconic German paddler, and one of the most decorated Olympic athletes of all time in any sport. She looked at me and shook her finger as if to challenge me, "not this time". That was all the motivation I needed to push harder. I decided I was going to beat her someday.

The very next summer, I was on top of the world and so was the entire women's team. I was winning world cups with the K4 team, and Marie-Josée Gibeau (Marie), my K2 partner, believed, along with me, that we were the fastest in the world. We trained and sprinted all season long, tallying up wins along the way in our crew boats and singles. I have never felt more trust and solid support than I did when I was racing with Marie. She was someone you wanted in your boat! I always knew that she would be IN. We battled and pushed each other in training camps and were the most fierce yet friendly teammates on the road. I owe a lot of my success to Marie and our many friendly battles. She and I raced our hearts out in 1998 in Szeged, Hungary—the heartland of sprint kayaking—at the World Championship regatta, and after winning our semi-final, we were seeded the fastest and given prime position in the middle of the lineup with the Hungarians on one side of us and the Germans on the other. This is an ideal spot to be in a race because you have a peripheral view of the whole field. It was the final race of the World Championships regatta and the final race of the season and I felt calm and confident. When the gun went off, Marie and I exploded out of our blocks and right away surged to the front of the pack. We were both fighters and we were the fastest off the starting line. We knew that if we got out in front, we would just get faster and faster by allowing the energy of the race to fuel our momentum. The crowd was deafeningly loud, and I don't think we heard each other the entire race, but we felt the full strength of our pushes and pulls together in perfect timing. We crossed the finish line in first place, ahead of the entire world! For the first time ever, we became World Champions together. What a feeling!

In 1999 I was racing with another partner, Caroline Brunet, who at the time was the number one K1 paddler in the world in the

500-metre race. She had asked me to train and race with her in the K2 at the World Championships in preparation for the Sydney Olympic Games, and I was honoured. In kayaking, the Olympic contenders are pre-qualified at the World Championships. Earning one of the few spots available here guarantees a country the right to enter a boat in the Olympic Games. If they don't qualify at the Worlds, there is always an outside option to get in through a hemispheric qualifier and compete against the South American countries and the USA. But it is always simplest to have this all sewn up at the Worlds.

Canada Qualifies!

Once the boat itself is qualified, the athletes still have to earn their own seat in it. This process is stressful and at times lengthy, and it comes down to a battle of wills. My "job" in 1999 was to help qualify Canada's K4 and K2 boats. Together, Caroline and I won a shining silver medal in the K2 500 metre race at the Worlds, guaranteeing that Canada would race that boat at the Olympic Games in Sydney, Australia. We still had to earn our individual seats in that boat by being the best Canadian crew in 2000 at the selection trials, however. I recall the moment after crossing the finish line on a chilly May afternoon in Montreal at the Olympic basin: I realized that I was indeed going to be an Olympian. I was overcome with emotion. Joy, excitement, pride, hope, fear. There was much more work to do on the journey, but I felt success and pride in my path. My family, my coach and my club had been my rocks and I felt their unwavering support and love, and I felt their pride.

In preparation for the Sydney Olympic Games, Caroline and I trained all over the world, stopping off at the Olympic Training centres in California, Florida, and Norway. It was intense travel. I was grateful for the opportunity, but I missed my home, my family, my coach and my club, as well as my Cheema training group. My soul was unhappy. I had also chosen to take only one course at university that winter due to my intense and prolonged travel. It was just Caroline and me together, every day and this was incredibly hard to take, mentally and physically. What I learned from that experience was the importance of being happy and experiencing enjoyment and fulfillment in what you're doing. If it becomes too much like work, then it gets really hard to find the motivation and momentum to keep going, day after day. I took that learning to heart in future years. For me, fulfillment is an important factor in my performance.

I remember learning a great deal from Caroline about how she approached the sport in a professional way. She was my mentor and I'd idolized her since I'd been a young kayak athlete. Her belief was big! She believed that she was the best. She taught me even more about myself and how to push myself harder. We pushed each other in the gym and on the water every day. I believe she revolutionized the sport of women's kayaking with her technique and knowledge of her stroke. Her fiercest rival was the German-born, Josefa Idem, who had married an Italian and was now racing for Italy. Caroline was strength and power, Josefa was grace and fluidity. They battled each other every race.

Olympic Games

The months flew by and finally I was in Sydney for the 2000 Olympic Games with the rest of the Canadian team, and I was ready to compete for my country. On the day of the Olympic finals, Caroline and I watched the wind out the window as we ate breakfast in our rented Canadian team house. The trees were moving a lot more than I'd ever seen before, thanks to hurricane force winds of 90 kilometres an hour. It was terrifying! It was also unheard of. The scene at the regatta centre at Penrith was chaotic, to say the least. Everything had to be tied down. The water was incredibly angry that day. Waves were crashing over the docks and safety boats were sinking. There was even talk of switching the direction of the race, so we could have a tail wind. We were called on and off the start line three times that day, which was unnerving. Each time, we were called to the line expecting an Olympic final to take place, only to have it called off to protect the safety of the athletes. I remember Caroline looking nervous and scared. I had never seen her like this before. Josefa talked to her about waging a protest and Caroline grabbed onto that thought for a few minutes. But that was not going to happen. This was the Olympic Final. It was the last day of the Games and the flame was to be extinguished that night at the closing ceremonies. The race was bound to happen. In extreme conditions, you have to make extreme preparations. I saw athletes carving their paddles to make them smaller, adjusting their boat set-up to be more stable in the waves, creating additional cockpit covers out of plastic bags to guard from the gale. These were extreme measures.

In the time between the numerous delays, I went over to the stands to visit my family: my two sisters and my mom and dad had made the trip to support me. I remember a defining moment with my dad. He always could tell when I was nervous and scared, and he said to me to give it my best and that they (my family) loved me anyway! It was a moment that I never will forget, and boy did I need that reassurance. Many times, I'd equate my personal value to my results where, in fact, I was still going to be me, win or lose and I would still have my family's unwavering love and support, win or lose. I'm so grateful for my family.

We finally pushed off from the dock for our final at 4:00 p.m., an hour after Caroline's K1 race, where she finished a soul-wrenching second place to Josefa. It was a race of historic proportions and I could tell Caroline was gutted. With an hour to go until our K2 Olympic final, I found Caroline lying on the ground on the floor of the boat bay. I chatted with her and tried to pump her up for our K2 race, telling her that we could do it together! Csom saw us off from the dock. He always had a way of just being there when I needed him. I remember paddling up the side of the course just wanting it to be over. I was scared, and I missed Caroline's strong spirit. I don't recall much about that Olympic race, but it was definitely Olympic. Waves crashed over the bow and we had to fight to keep from falling into the water. The water was freezing cold and our boat was bouncing. We were neck and neck with three other crews, fighting for an Olympic medal, but we finished fifth. Fifth felt like a failure. I felt physically, mentally, and emotionally empty. Worst of all, I felt that I had let everyone down. Especially the kids back home at my canoe club, who were having a sleepover at Cheema so they could watch me compete. I held that feeling for a few minutes while we cooled down and brought our boat to the media dock. I recall thinking to myself that I wanted to share something with the kids back home. I wanted to connect with the young girls who were watching that race live. What came out of my mouth were words to the effect that this was part of the journey and that in difficult or challenging times you have to mine for the gold in the journey. The gold is there, buried in the dirt at times. The Gold is the journey...That thinking completely changed my life and the course of my sport career moving forward. The gold is in the journey! It is a phrase I live by every day and I offer it to you.

The next summer, my goal was to take the K1 spot in Canada and race that event at the World Championships. I was on top at all the world cup races that year with many best-ever results, and being part of a winning and well-managed team was always an important part of my success. We pushed each other on and off the water and the success of our women's team in the early 2000s was in large part due to the combined effort of each athlete, our coach, Csom, and our team leadership and support staff. We got to train in Munich prior to the World Championships. Life is easy at training camp. We sleep, we eat, we train, we repeat. Each day, I felt faster and lighter on the water. The World Championships were in Poznan, Poland, in 2001 and, on the final day, I was racing the K1 200-metre, my favorite event. I remember lining up for that race feeling totally calm and ready, and there was a tiny little tail wind. Conditions were ideal for me to go fast! I blasted off the start line and felt a slight lead right from the first five strokes! I never lost that lead and ended up winning the event—my second world championship title—and I did it in world record time! I have had very few perfect races in my 20-year career. This one was perfect and special, and I felt so proud! I remember looking up at the scoreboard and seeing my name flash first!

The Canadian Anthem Played

I felt extremely confident and comfortable sprinting that whole season. It was what I was born to do. Standing on the top step of the podium is a feeling that I will never forget. It meant the world to me to hear the Canadian anthem played in my honour, with my family and teammates and coach there with me. As I sang the words, I started to cry a happy, heartful cry. I spotted my family among the thousands of fans in the grandstands. I wanted that moment to last forever.

The 2005 racing season was probably the busiest of my entire life. I was racing three different K1 distances at the World Championships, 200-metre, 500-metre and 1000-metre. I won medals in all three for my best season ever! I was getting married that fall and I was defending my master's thesis at Dalhousie University on the determinants of effective coaches. It was a fun research topic for me. More than anything, I was happy. But busy was the name of the game! My fiancé, Jeremy, and I were happy, and we felt like a good team. I had met him at university and got to know him as a friend. We started dating right after the 2004 Athens Olympic Games and started planning for our future. He is a special guy, and he challenged me to think about things differently. He helped me dig deeper into who I am and helped me find different areas of strength and growth. He helped me hone my recovery skills and take my training to the next level of greatness. We started I Promise Performance which we grew together for a couple of years. Jeremy is a big part of who I am today. We were married for eight years and although we are no longer married, we still remain friends and I am grateful for the chance to have him in my life. Jeremy now owns a company called Athletigen that tests genetic markers for athletic potential, nutritional requirements and injury, etc. This is truly the future of program precision for athletes and teams.

I raced for 17 years all around the world as a member of the national sprint team and today I still rely on many power processes every day that I developed during my years as a competitor. My workouts, my nutrition, sleep habits, self-care and my daily routine...I rarely miss executing on any of the factors that I know add up to success for me. I know the impact on my body and my energy if I do miss and, more importantly now, I understand the importance of "showing up" for my company, my clients and my conference work. I still enjoy days off every week, but I rely on my process to help me function and perform at my best.

Learning to love myself through failure, and gaining wisdom along the way to the wins, has been the biggest area of growth for me. With anything, you have to have fun while failing first. No one starts out with winning. Just as in training, you must embrace the pain points and be willing to dig into them to explore your sources of strength from that place. The pureness of racing uncovers that, and for that I am grateful. It is in those "step up" moments that we learn the most about ourselves. There is no substitute for being on the line, with fear in your belly, and breathing through it anyway to find calm water and sacred space in the moment. There is no fast track to success. You have to just be, and be willing to travel through whatever life holds for you.

No One Hits All Their Goals

Despite the many "quick solutions" that often bombard us online and in popular media, no one starts out as a world class performer, speaker, writer, player, teammate, or business person. No one hits all their goals. In fact, the goal can at times limit us, allowing us to see only that one thing in our direct vision. By contrast, if we gently hold the goal in our awareness and allow other goals, options, and paths to also present themselves, we can appreciate the journey so much more. Passion gets you started, but it is the dedication to the process, the persistence with it, and the patience that gets you through. Being open to the path ahead, and the insights that it offers, is the most important piece of the journey. And, if you're willing to travel the slow, scenic route, you will be ever more enlightened by what you find.

I had a meaningful conversation with an artist at one of my recent conferences. She explained how artists approach process differently from most athletes, in that they have no goal at the outset. Their work is all about being immersed in the process of what they are doing. The actual "goal" of creating is to let things unfold as they will. That conversation reaffirmed my advice for young athletes: focus and trust in the process, and allow yourself to end up at a whole new destination.

My power process is my daily routine and I rely on it for my success. I allow slight deviations to it, but, generally, it functions as a script. It was pretty tough to define my process after I retired from sport. I felt for a long while that I had nothing to prepare for. It didn't take long to figure out that I couldn't perform the way I wanted to if I got too little sleep or neglected to take care of myself. I later realized that my process for performance is even more important now because I interact with so many more people. (I will share my transition experience in a later chapter.) I now plan ahead for times when I can't follow my normal routine. For example, when I travel, I bring my gym gear and outdoor running gear, as well as my nutritional supplements and my favorite water bottle. Sometimes, I even bring my favorite pillow so that I can get a good night's sleep!

You can put my POWER processes to work on behalf of your goals as well, and here's what you can do to start creating your day in a positive, empowering way:

Present Moment Awareness

Becoming present helps us to gather the right information and make the right decisions.

The first step in this process is to check in with how you're feeling and how you're being. You can then set an intention and acknowledge that you are committing to yourself. Any decision you make from this perspective is based on YOU and your values and this is a key part of learning to put yourself first. The skill here is to become aware of your breathing. Notice it, and become present to it. No matter what happens, we will always be present if we come back to our breath. Inhale for a count of four and exhale for a count of four. Notice any feelings or dialogue that come up for you and, if they do, that's OK. Gently shift your awareness back to the movement of breath through your body.

If you want a deeper feeling of relaxation, focus on inhaling for seven counts and exhaling for 11. This will reduce muscle tension and anxiety, activating the parasympathetic nervous system. The key is to focus on only your breath. It is not that you cannot have other thoughts. But if they arise, simply watch them like clouds or waves floating by, and gently bring the focus back to your breath.

Remember that we can be our own worst enemy if we don't train our mind, and we can act unconsciously to undermine ourselves. The fact is, somedays we just don't wake up with good energy, and the day can get the best of us. Far better is for us to get the best out of the day.

Here's a tool to help align your mind first thing in the morning:

1. When you first wake up, breathe in and out and say one-to-three positive things to yourself. Examples could be:

- "Who do I choose to be today?"
- "Today, I choose to be awesome and anything is possible."
- "Here's how I envision success for me today…"
- "This is my moment."

- "I am filled with possibility."
- "I embrace this day with all its challenges."

2. Spend some time reflecting on gratitude. Write or think of one-to-three things, people, and/or experiences you're grateful for. Here's the key: One of them must be, or be about YOU.

3. Visualize your day, event, race, presentation, routine, or rehearsal unfolding as you want it to unfold, and then feel it. You actually want to pretend that it has already occurred, and it is now in the past. Feel the feelings of having had success in the day with what you have done. When you play this scene in your mind, you are actually engaging your brain to create the energy that you need to make it happen! It works! Then your job is to come back to the present moment and get yourself ready to perform. You still have to make it all happen. You still have to do the work.

4. Write your values, goals or intentions in a journal and determine what you will focus on today to move one step closer to them. What will be your big WIN today? Start small.

To help with this, I use the acronym, "WIN." It stands for: What's Important Now. Ask yourself that question and decide on what your wins are for the day. This may help guide your reflections afterwards, or set your intentions going forward.

You also might want to find clippings, words, and images of what inspires you. Or create a photo journal or a blog. Regardless of how you do it, record your wins and celebrate your victories! Every day has at least one win in it. Start identifying and recognizing each one. Read your journal and write in it, first thing in the morning and last thing at night before you sleep. It doesn't have to be a huge project. But it needs to happen most days of the week. It helps you to stay focused and moving towards your goals. It also helps to identify areas of strength and areas for improvement. Perhaps start with a gratitude piece. What are you grateful for right now?

For your own copy of the Power Process and the Situation Creator tools, go to: strongbeauty.ca

Connecting to intention brings clarity, connection, focus and purpose.

CHAPTER 4: "O" is for Opening to Receive

In my post-graduate work, I had the opportunity to be trained in Acceptance Commitment Therapy or ACT. The premise of ACT is that we benefit from choosing to engage in committed action that honours our unique values. The skill here is to be aware of all emotions. Notice where you might feel a particular emotion in your body? Ask how old that emotion may be. When we are aware of our feelings, we can choose whether or not to act in accordance with them. All emotions are simply energy in motion. Letting them be part of you, and not a definition of who you are, is key to managing them while living a fulfilling life in line with your values. Especially with emotions such as fear, it is important to recognize them, and hold them gently by acknowledging them; be grateful for all of your emotions. Soften, soothe and allow.

Emotional awareness is key to being able to broaden our perception and our perspective. We can choose whether to act on our emotions or not. All emotions are OK and we each experience and process emotions and energy in our own way. So, honour that. But know that you can drive and shift your own perception if you need to or want to. Ask yourself: "Is this helpful?" Or, "Is this working for me?" Sometimes negative emotions can stop us from experiencing our greatest potential by keeping us stuck. Sometimes we need to just get out of our own way and let our greatness shine. Focus on present moment awareness, and something that might make you feel present, connected or peaceful. It might be a situation that you remember, a person or something inanimate, like a sunset or a rainbow or a familiar sight. Focus on engaging that feeling in your heart; be open to receive without judgement.

Self-Talk: Creating Power Words and Mantras

Our connection to our words is a reflection of what is going on inside our minds. Choosing our words carefully and intentionally has a tremendous effect on our own energy, as well as those around us.

After recording all of my day's training sessions every day I used to write in my training journal: "I am the fastest!", or "I am so fast!" and I would draw a sprint kayaker alongside that sentence. It was my mantra and I believed it. Every day for 15 years, I would create those words and feel the feelings that came along with those words. I dared to think it, and write it, and then, before long, I believed it!

You can create any reality that you desire for yourself. You just have to dare to think and feel it. Consider for a moment your own self-talk. Have you ever been nervous or scared about an upcoming performance, tryout, or even a speech? I know I have! I've also caught myself saying some pretty hurtful things, TO MYSELF!

A little self-criticism is a good thing, but we need to keep it in check when that voice becomes too harsh. Instead of focusing on your shortcomings or "failures," turn that thinking around and focus instead on the small improvements you have made. Studies show that over the long term, self-trash-talk can lead to higher stress and depression (Chansky, Freeing Yourself From Anxiety). A good rule of thumb is to remember to treat yourself as you would treat others and treat others as you wish to be treated.

That starts with our words, our emotions and our body language. Try this: Develop a few positive words or statements to counter some of your typical negative thoughts or self-talk statements and to open yourself to a more abundant way of being in the world. This develops a skill in reframing your thoughts. Focusing on using the more positively-framed thought or statement or word automatically creates a new neural highway in the brain that can quickly become a preferred route and it will put you on the road to more positive thoughts in no time!

Keep a few key phrases laminated in your gym bag for quick reading when you need to spark your positive thinking for a Strong Beauty moment!

Here is a five-point framework to help you with this:

1. **The Power of Possible Thinking.** According to Tamar Chansky, PhD., her research shows we often feel a lot of pressure to turn our thoughts around and make them positive, which can backfire and actually make us feel worse. Instead,

she suggests we reach for neutral thoughts about a situation, and stick to the facts.

2. **What would my best friend say?** A quick way to re-direct negative self-talk is to consider the situation from the more gentle approach of a friend. A good rule of thumb: If you wouldn't say it to your best friend, don't say it to yourself.

3. **Give your inner critic a name.** Brené Brown, PhD., is the author of the popular book, The Gifts of Imperfection. She says that if you give your inner critic a name, preferably a silly one, it helps break the hold it has on you. Examples are the Perfectionist, or the Gremlin.

4. **Give your rants a name, too.** Your rants and your stories only get energy when you choose to fuel them. Giving yourself a bird's eye view of them helps keep things in perspective. Examples: the "My friends are better than me" story, the "Poor me" story, and the "I never get anything done" story. Thoughts and stories are also habits. If you want your energy to change, start telling yourself a different story!

5. **Embrace imperfection.** It is super-freeing to cut yourself a little slack and not hold yourself to incredibly high standards. I learned this as an athlete and as a speaker, and I trained myself to just dive in and give my best. Perfection is impossible, but giving your very best effort, honouring where you are, and being willing to build momentum by potentially messing up and moving on will always serve you well!

Learning to Overcome Common Thinking Traps

There are some common thinking-related traps a lot of us fall into but it's relatively easy to get out of them. The trick is to remember to put them to work for us. Here are some examples of how this works:

Polarized Thinking

You see things as black or white, good or bad, wrong or right, always or never. "I need to get 100% or I've failed myself (or others)." A good reframing thought to plant is to ask the question: "Is this true?"

Catastrophizing

You expect disaster, even picture it. You notice a problem and ask, "What if…?". A good reframe of this thinking is to focus on what you can control. Certain things just aren't worth our energy and worry. Bring your attention back into the present.

Magnifying

You "turn up the volume" on anything bad and make it loud, large or overwhelming. To reframe this thinking, think of something positive and turn up the volume on it instead.

Minimizing

You make positive things less important than they are. Instead of thinking that your assets, such as your ability to cope and find solutions, are not good enough, imagine all the times in your life when you felt successful and positive.

The "Shoulds"

You have a strict list of rules about how you and other people should act. You may criticize yourself when you don't live up to your expectations. Example: "I should be studying." "I should never feel certain emotions, such as anger or jealousy." Time to be a little more gentle with YOU. "Shoulds" just come from that inner critic and they can be very harsh and harmful. They creep up when we change our behaviour and habits for something new. Instead of listening to the "I Shoulds," focus on an "I Am…" statement. Stick to the facts and evoke a feeling of gratitude. I experienced more gentleness and acceptance of myself when I eliminated the word "should" and replaced it with "could" in my language. I am conscious of it through a fun little challenge I did.

Mind Reading

Without their input, you believe you know how other people are feeling and why they act the way they do. In particular, you think you know how people think and feel about you—even though you have no proof. Example: "Everyone thinks I'm stupid." This one comes up for me a lot when I'm faced with presenting to groups. To reframe this thinking trap, imagine all the positive things about you and the people around you. Ask yourself, "how can I help?" and "what do I need in this moment?" If you start appreciating the people around you, and begin to hold that for yourself, your experience in the moment will change, I Promise.

Personalization

You think that everything people do or say is some kind of reaction to you. You compare yourself to others. "She is smarter (or more competent, better looking, etc.) than I am." Your team loses, and you think, "It's all my fault that we lost." Reframe that thinking instead to include the strengths and the unique values that you bring to the table!

Filtering (tunnel vision)

You focus on the negative details, while ignoring all the positive aspects of a situation. "I didn't get the MVP award." (Although you did receive other awards or recognition). Focus on what you have done and the journey you've taken to bring you to right now. Hold appreciation for that experience, for yourself and for everyone who helped you get to where you are now.

Overgeneralization

You make broad conclusions based on a single incident or piece of evidence. One bad experience means that whenever you are in a similar situation, the result will be bad. Reframe this thought by coming into the present and knowing that each moment is unique, and you bring all your experiences and knowledge to the creation of a new moment.

Fortune Telling

You predict the future, usually with a high likelihood of a negative outcome. You think "I know I'm going to fail that test," even when you have been studying and the chances of failing are low. To reframe this, remember that no one can predict the future, but you certainly can prepare for it with your processes and systems. Let the future unfold and trust that you've done all that you can to be in the place that you are.

Emotional Reasoning

You base your views of things on what you are feeling, rather than what is really going on. You feel tired and unhappy, so you think "My life totally sucks."

Labelling

You call yourself names instead of just describing an event or behaviour. Example: If you make a mistake, you call yourself a "stupid loser" instead of just telling yourself that you made an error. Take the harsh labels out of the situation and instead use language such as: "I'm having the thought that...", or "I'm feeling...". Recognize that when you have an emotional reaction to a state of mind or an event you are not defining who you are. This is key to helping yourself in a moment of adversity.

Coping statements remind you that you are able to handle a situation and have ways to deal with problems. They need to be personal and directly applicable to the situation that is causing your anxiety in order to work well, and lower your anxiety.

Example: Anxious Thought Coping Statements

You have the thought "I'm never going to get any better at this..." stuck in your head. Replace this thought with:

"I'm making daily progress toward my goal of ______. It takes time and effort to achieve this success."

Or; "I've made changes before, I can do it again."

Or, "I'm experiencing a setback. This is a normal part of the process along the path to my goal of ______."

Or, "I'm not alone. People care about me and they are going to support me through this."

Here are some strong, positive, statements to keep in your back pocket for when you need some help staying open to possibility:

- There is no need to panic.
- I can get through this.
- It doesn't need to be perfect.
- My best is good enough.
- Just breathe out and relax.
- This feeling isn't comfortable or pleasant, but I can accept it.
- I can feel anxious and still deal with this situation.
- This will pass.

- I'll ride through this.
- I don't need to let this get to me.
- I can choose to think differently.
- Balance.
- I have time for me.
- I deserve a break.
- I am brave.
- One step at a time.
- Will this matter in 10 years?
- I am not alone.
- I am exactly where I need to be.
- I can ask for help.
- I matter.
- I'm an inspiration.
- Dream big.
- I learn something new every day.
- Each step is up to me…
- I can trust my intuition.
- My life is up to me.
- I make good choices.
- I make strong, healthy, smart decisions.
- It's a new day.
- I have time for me.

Overcoming Motivational Blocks

Blocks to motivation can leave us feeling unmotivated, de-energized and out of control. Scientific American identifies three blocks to motivation:

1. Feeling forced
2. Finding the activity pointless
3. Doubting our capability

Taking on one of these blocks can help you feel more empowered around your goals and ability to get things done! Can you identify which block typically gets in the way for you?

Which stories are you telling yourself that may be undermining your performance?

Congratulations, and give yourself a pat on the back! Identifying that you're being blocked is key to building awareness. Once you're aware, beware! Now you can do something about it.

The key to overcoming motivational blocks is to make a small movement forward on the task. One action will change your momentum and provide you with some steam to keep motivated.

If you're feeling forced, perhaps add language such as: "I choose to…"

Do you feel as though an activity is pointless? Try brainstorming all the benefits you will receive if you do the task, i.e. cleaning your apartment or your room may seem pointless, but is it really?

Having feelings of self-doubt around your capabilities? Try researching ideas on how to complete your task, or ask for help.

Moving just a little bit further towards the completion of a task helps to build energy. Engage with how you're feeling when you actually get started. We often build a task up in our minds, making it seem like much more effort than it actually is.

Make a list of the little things that you can organize in order to make a small start on your task and just start! Spending five uninterrupted minutes is better than putting it off and procrastinating further. Developing that self-discipline is an important skill to getting things done. Celebrate that WIN!

Strengthen your roots and believe in your growth.

CHAPTER 5: "W" is for Wisdom

Recognize that you have strength, and notice where you are when you are in a position of strength. Just take a moment and appreciate all that you are and what you have come through during your journey to this point. There is wisdom in that. There is wisdom in each of your cells. They all know how you perform best. Spend a moment in gratitude for yourself and the people in your world, perhaps those who have helped you to be here right now. There is wisdom in you.

Honouring the journey means taking a look at your path and how far you've traveled in relation to your starting point. It also means taking a closer look at your habits and processes. Take a moment to appreciate your own unique path, and know that you've gained wisdom from that journey.

What does your current power process look and feel like? Perhaps a power process for you might be to:

- Read a chapter from a book every day to ignite your reading skills
- Cultivate some prime internal time by turning off your phone and spending less time on your social media accounts

- Practice an instrument for half an hour, four days a week, to improve your musical skills
- Practice speaking up in a group setting, or with your close friends, if you wish to improve your public speaking
- Practice journalling or writing every day if you want to improve your writing skills
- Do five math problems each day to improve what you're working on in math class

Practice anything by breaking a skill down into its component parts. Example: racing starts in kayaking. Break the task into a focused first stroke that practices your balance and timing. Then practice the first four-to-six strokes to focus on building power and momentum. Then put it all together to practice the full start. Power processes are just the systems of success by which you can get at your goals.

Other power processes for goals could be:

Goal: Write and publish a book.

Power Process: 20 minutes daily of focused, free-form writing.

I invite you to take a moment to reflect again on the S.M.A.R.T.E.R goals that you've already created. Revisit them and consider your energy when you interact with them. Think about what your current power systems are, and write them down. What gets you to where you want to BE each day? Your power process can help you when you are feeling overwhelmed by your big goals.

Recognize and appreciate where you have strength and where you can improve just a little bit in your success systems. Own it. Know that going through this process is the first step in activating it!

One of the first times I realized this for myself was when I set out to bench press 220 pounds of weights one day at my gym. I have always loved how strong and powerful I feel in the gym, and I love the energy I feel when I'm there. It's where I can experience my most pure self. I had gone through my regular warm-up that day and I was feeling ready to do my lift. I had set a big goal and my coach was spotting me. I had already created my lift so vividly in my mind that I felt like I'd already successfully completed it. There was a lot of weight on the bar and my goal was to lift it off the rack, bring it down to my chest and push it straight up and back to the rack.

I thought about the fact that I had a huge amount of strength because of all the work I'd been doing in the gym. I felt completely ready. I exhaled forcefully three times, placed my hands on the knurled grips of the bar, and I went for it! I was All In! I couldn't believe the mindset that I was in, and had to be in, for that lift. I recognized the wisdom of my body immediately: every motor neuron and pathway was activated to exact precision. The Golgi tendon organs in the belly of my pecs and elsewhere on my arms and back were activating in pure synchronicity to create this extreme power movement. I completed the lift beautifully! I knew at that moment that I had unleashed a power wiser than I'd ever known before. The combination of mindset, heartset, and bodyset, powered by the intention of connected energy, is virtually unstoppable.

The cool thing is that you don't need all the stars to align to create this intention of energy. You just need to activate and believe in it.

Photo by Alexandr Grebelnik on Unsplash

The Power of Habits

Our habits are an essential ingredient to our success. In fact, I would go as far as stating that:

Habits + Conscious, Persistent Daily Effort = Success!

Do you want to become the kind of person who puts their best self forward and actively chooses to be their best every day? Who believes in themselves? Who can be counted on by the people that matter to you? If so, I encourage you to remember that the daily habits and processes that you follow are more important than the ultimate goal you are seeking to achieve.

Why is this true? Your life today is essentially the sum of your habits. Today, you are exactly where you need to be to grow from here...

Your experience of fitness and health? They're the result of your physical activity, nutritional and self-care habits.

Your experiences of happiness? They are derived from your thoughts and mental habits.

Your experience with success? It's generated by your approach to your goals and your power process habits.

Keep in mind that it's the little things you do every day that help you get from where you are today to where you want to go....

I'm a big believer in the value of improving by just a small amount every day. Over time, this will help you generate significant gains and along the way will allow you to build the foundation for high performance in whatever it is you're working to achieve. Steady habits and the power of small, significant choices add up over time.

More significant still is the fact that what you repeatedly do (i.e. what you spend time thinking about and doing each day) ultimately forms the person you are, the things you believe, and the personality that you present to the world. Think about how you spend your time and determine if that aligns with your big goals. Because you only get one shot to make today great!

The most common mistake that people make is setting their sights on an event, a transformation, or an overnight success they want to achieve – rather than focusing on their habits and routines and the slow climb to success that greatness requires. Always bring your goals back down to Earth and the path on which you're currently ascending. Where is your next step? Can you identify it? What can you do right NOW?

I've been guilty of this just like everyone else. And today, I'm still learning how to master my habits, just like you.

Self-Confidence and Belief

Every habit or action you perform is driven by a belief. If you change your beliefs about the type of person you are (and yes, you can shift that construct whenever you wish), then it's easier to change your habits and actions to actively create a new identity, perhaps one that includes a greater level of self-confidence.

Underlying all of this is the importance of building strong habits and success systems. New habits and actions can build even bigger beliefs. How big is your dream?

The reason it's so hard to stick to new habits is that we often try to achieve a performance – or appearance – based goal without changing our concept of who we are. Focus on changing your beliefs first. There is a theory called the Pygmalion effect which describes this. Here's how it works:

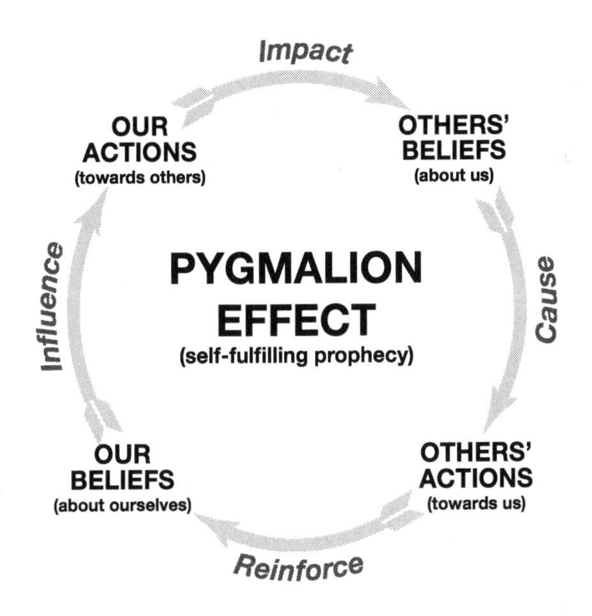

The premise of this theory is that the expression of who we are starts in our mind first. If you want to change who you are and how you show up in the world, then you have to first change the belief or the story you have about who you are.

What are the relevant beliefs or stories in your life? What conversations are you having? Is there an area in your life you want to change, or evolve, or something around which you would like to develop a new storyline? Take some time to write about this.

Learning Opportunity:

Write down some new beliefs that you want to embrace, or three-to-five power statements (mantras) with which you want to align. Repeat them in your mind or aloud so that they gain strength. The more you do this, the more effectively you will change your beliefs. Here's the cool part…You can choose absolutely anything!

Expanding and growing requires us to find new ways to push ourselves. Pushing yourself out of your comfort zone and experiencing new levels of discomfort teaches you a lot about what you can tolerate, and you can in turn discover new strengths and skills that you can draw upon. One of the things our coach told us was that if we always trained at the same speed, we would never know how fast we can go!

The Three-Step Recipe for Sustained Success:

Changing your beliefs isn't nearly as hard as you might think. There are three steps involved:

1. Decide who you want to be in relation to your goals.

2. Write it down and practice saying it to yourself over and over.

3. Reinforce and prove it to yourself through your behaviours, and in the small wins you experience each day.

Reconnect with Your Successes and Feel-Good Moments

In order to build confidence, athletes reconnect with or recall their previous successes. In the build-up to a big championship race, I would regularly remind myself of all my best training sessions, previous races, world cup and world championship victories. I would bring to the forefront of my mind all of the great performances I had delivered. I would also remind myself of all of the fast time controls (race simulations) I had been doing recently. This process would build my self-belief, hence my confidence.

Later on in my career, I learned the value of connecting with feel-good moments. I learned the power of stepping outside of the thoughts that accompanied me into the competition arena for a moment and recalling a feel-good moment. This would often put my mind and nerves at ease. My mantra was Breathe, Smile and Trust. Those words brought about mental ease for me. When I was in a state of mental ease, I could perform better.

Next time you find yourself feeling a little bit anxious about an upcoming performance or challenging situation, take a few moments to reconnect with some of your previous successes or feel-good moments. Perhaps recall the last time that you were in a situation and dealt with it well, or maybe a similar challenge that you excelled at, and can give you confidence now.

Eventually, all the preparations are complete, and it's time for your performance, big game or important event. Many people think that the athlete or team who wants it the most on the day of the competition is the one who wins, as if belief alone will make it happen. We need to change that way of thinking.

Belief and positive thought are big parts of success, and they will get us through the tough training moments. When it comes to the big game day, however, our focus needs to shift from outcome and external motivation, to inner power. What do we need to do and focus on to be at our best? We need to focus on the behaviours and thoughts that create our best performances. Present moment awareness and focus on the small details of how we can get to our optimum level, stroke by stroke, are key.

When I was competing, my focus had to be on consistently transferring my body weight onto the blade of my paddle. That allowed me to create the most powerful and quick strokes through the water possible. And I had to evoke a feeling of happiness, goodness. I would smile... I knew that when I was able to do that, I could effectively create my top speed for the whole race. When I was able to do that, I was paddling at my best. It was something that I practiced and rehearsed daily. It seems relatively simple. But when it comes down to delivering on The Day, you have to think of very little, and clear your mind of noise so that you can focus on the process, not the outcome. The details are key. Victories are achieved one tiny process at a time, in centimetres and millimetres.

I recall reading an article from a member of the Canadian women's national rugby sevens team at the Rio Olympic Games. A victory for the Canadians at the start of the final day seemed like such a mammoth task that focusing on the outcome would have been overwhelming. Instead, each and every member of the team went out to play the game of their lives, focused on one play at a time, one try at a time, knowing that the result they desired just might follow. Even when the Canadians were trailing, they kept focusing on each individual play, and stayed present to the game. Play by play, the Canadian girls were able to equalize the score and force an overtime, which ultimately resulted in a victory and an Olympic bronze medal. When it's time to execute your own winning performance, remember to focus on the process, and ask yourself, "What is the power process here that is going to help me achieve my outcome?"

Performance and Process Assessment Tool

The final element in generating further success is to do a self-assessment after each race, performance or event, and then ask someone you trust to sit down with you and co-assess how it went. You want to do this with someone who will give you honest feedback and even challenge your thinking, and I suggest you use guided questions to frame the discussion. Perhaps start with a review of what went well and what didn't go so well, and examine how you felt and how you want to feel going forward.

Most importantly, come up with a game plan to help you in the next race or in your next event, one that is based on what you learned from the performance you've just finished.

How often do you take time to reflect on a performance or a project? Perhaps use the Performance and Process Assessment Tool after your next performance!

Download your copy of the Process Assessment Tool on the website, strongbeauty.ca

Ask for Feedback

A key element of the review stage is giving and receiving feedback. Feedback can come from teachers, or tests you've taken in school. In the business world, feedback is sometimes given at an annual review or at the proposal stage of a project. As an athlete, I couldn't wait to solicit feedback until the end of the season; I needed weekly, if not daily feedback and check-ins, otherwise, I could be engaging in sub-optimal routines for 12 months! If I wanted to constantly improve—and build my confidence—I needed frequent feedback and regular conversations about how I could keep improving.

I would ask for feedback from all of the different people on my team – sports scientists and psychologists, my coach, our massage therapist, etc. When I was on the water, I got feedback from my GPS and my heart-rate monitor, while I was also getting input cues from my coach on my technique and my stroke rate. I'd also ask for feedback after every session. I knew that every bit of feedback represented a competitive advantage designed to make me better at my sport. This was one of the most challenging things I found in my transition from sport into my next career. I noticed that I perform better with feedback, so I had to put myself in professional situations and mastermind groups where I knew I'd receive feedback, as well as be able to offer my input.

How often do you seek feedback?

If you're a leader on your team, how often do you give feedback?

The key to giving or receiving feedback is to treat it as an objective and valuable piece of information. It is in no way a direct reflection on you, as a person. Sometimes it's hard to make that distinction, but I Promise that, if you can do that, you will surely meet your goals faster! Your coach—and anyone else giving feedback—undoubtedly tries to communicate in a manner that will engage you at the highest level of integrity possible, just like any other performance team. So, instead of framing feedback as something negative, look at it as an "area of opportunity for improvement." Or another "opportunity to gather information." Think of the feedback as a little seed that will help you grow stronger, a little golden nugget!

Constructive Criticism Versus Positive Feedback

Imagine if I sat on the start line of the World Championships thinking about my limitations and the behaviours I needed to avoid? I wouldn't have a hope of performing at my best! In fact, if I focused on my weaknesses and what not to do, chances are, I would perform the "what-not-to-do" really well! Instead, my coach would regularly give me feedback on my strengths: he would highlight my skills and abilities, so I could work to make them even stronger. That was far more valuable than trying to bring my weaknesses up to par: it helped build positive self-belief, so I could perform at my best.

How easily can you list the strengths, and other qualities that you bring to your team?

Try this exercise in your journal:

My Strengths:

1. ______________________________

2. ______________________________

3. ______________________________

4. ______________________________

5. ______________________________

Areas of Opportunity for Improvement:

1. ______________________________

2. ______________________________

3. ______________________________

4. ______________________________

5. ______________________________

So, the message is, in order to develop a winning mindset, adopt an athlete mindset. Slow down, take some time to prepare for events, and then review your performance afterwards. View this as an investment of time that will enhance your performance.

Download your copy of the Strengths and Opportunities tool at strongbeauty.ca

---

Here Are My Seven Keys to Developing an Inner Athlete Mindset:

1. Take time to prepare physically and mentally; honour, respect and protect this time.
2. Reconnect with your previous successes in order to build self-belief and engage confidence.
3. Focus on the power process, not the outcome, when it comes time to perform.
4. Reflect on a performance through conversation and journalling, and uncover the lessons that can be learned.
5. Seek feedback often.
6. Focus on your strengths.
7. Outline your opportunities for improvement and devote some time to growing in those areas.

There is so much potential energy within you.

CHAPTER 6: "E" is for Energy and Intention

We choose where we focus our energy. This is really important to understand. We choose! People can try to influence you, but ultimately you are the navigator of your boat. I Promise that the decisions you make about how you spend your energy—combined with your attitude towards the situations that you encounter—will make a big difference in your efforts to live a fulfilling life.

Positive expectations, and goals with good milestones and checkpoints, will also help keep you on track. I like to think of goals as forming a pathway up a mountain. You have one big, lofty goal, and you really want to reach it. So, you must engage it within you. Start devoting energy to it. Read about it, write it down and cut messages about it out of magazines and online resources, and recognize the information that you encounter in the world that supports your quest to achieve it.

As with any journey, there are always challenges to overcome and points along the path that are difficult, but the key is to keep climbing and moving forward toward your goal for as long as it resonates with you. One step at a time. Momentum, forward movement and a positive attitude serve to reconfirm your motivation and your energy. They deepen and strengthen the neural pathways in our brains and hearts. By the same token, negative energy neural pathways can also become entrenched. So, choose a positive pattern of energy to enhance your physiology.

When all is said and done, managing your energy and regulating your emotions will help you to win like an Olympian!

Positive Emotions Fuel Your Brain for Peak Performance

In the winter of 2007, I found myself dealing with some difficulties in my relationship. I tried to maintain my smile and my work ethic during training but, on the inside, I was struggling, and I was paying a price. No matter what I did, I could not shake the feeling that something was wrong and that Jeremy, my partner, was having a tough time. Because he was struggling, so was I. This had been going on for years and finally, in 2007, I decided that I had to learn some new skills to cope with the situation and, at the same time, be of greater support to Jeremy.

I went to a workshop on mental skills —the area I had studied for my master's degree—that was hosted by our regional sport centre. At that workshop, a man by the name of Dirk Stroda, who is now a colleague of mine, introduced me to the work of the HeartMath Institute and it changed my life. For the first time in a long while, I began to feel positive about my ability to manage stress and assist others around me. The whole premise of the HeartMath philosophy is that when we focus on positive emotions, we generate, and surround ourselves with, a more positive energy field. This energy field has a direct impact on our performance and on other people around us. Whoa! Now that was a huge Aha moment for me! It helped me take ownership of my own energy field, and helped me understand my responses to things that had happened in my life.

I wondered if I could have been contributing to the distress that Jeremy was feeling? For the first time, I decided to look inward. After long sessions of meditation and deep breathing, I realized that I was concerned that Jeremy couldn't love me. That he would leave. I was emitting an energy of fear and I was feeling it as stress. As I learned how to feel love for myself and feel beauty from within, all those feelings of fear seemed to dissipate. The surprising part was that when I focused on gratitude and beauty, and felt happy inside, I paddled faster and with greater ease! WOW!

I realized this amazing institute in California was onto something of great value to everyone in our fast-paced, highly-stressed world. I had experienced high levels of stress in my athletic career and my relationship challenges, and I was excited about learning a skill set that would better allow me to become more proactive in dealing with this challenging issue. I travelled to the HeartMath Institute in Boulder Creek, California, to study its program more intensely, and I met all of the organization's founders and researchers. I was so impressed I decided to invest deeply in my own HeartMath training, with the ultimate goal of obtaining my certification and license. The Institute is located in a beautiful retreat setting among the massive redwood trees of northern California, and during my training I felt embraced by the surroundings and the entire community. I learned how to breathe, opening my body and heart to regulate my own emotions, and how to heal old emotional scars. I saw a great deal of value in this skill, for myself and for others. Little did I know at the time that this trip, this one choice, this adventure, would change the course of my career in sport—and now my business—forever.

The same skills that I learned at the HeartMath Institute travelled with me to many start lines and podiums over the years, and they are still part of my daily practice today.

The Amygdala Hijack

The amygdala is an almond-shaped mass in the temporal lobe of our brain. It is involved in our motivation and many of our emotional reactions, most significantly in those related to survival. At the HeartMath Institute, I started learning about the amygdala and how it can short circuit during times of emotional stress. It flips quite easily into fight-or-flight mode, which explains why I'd freeze or freak out when giving presentations early in my school years and on start lines as an athletic competitor. In times of perceived danger, we are all naturally wired to fight, flight or freeze. This keeps us out of imminent danger but it "hijacks" our behaviour so we don't necessarily act rationally.

Imagine you are attending an event that has triggered an intense negative emotional response (fear, anger, jealousy, anxiety, etc.).

This activates the amygdala and then triggers the fight-or-flight response to keep you safe. You have probably already felt what it's like to go into panic mode! The problem is that this amygdala hijack can last three-to-four hours. Our bio-system is filled with neurochemicals and hormones that encourage us to continue down that spiral pathway for quite a while, preventing our rational, calm mind from getting back in control. Have you ever gotten into an argument right before bed and then found that you couldn't sleep? When we are aware of this stress response, we can proactively prepare ourselves to deal with it through mindfulness and meditation. This helps prime our physiology to use our biology.

When I started learning that I could stop this emotional "amygdala hijack" if I wanted to, I gained mental strength.

Here's what to do in the heat-of-the-moment:

1. Realize what's going on: "Beware or Be Aware." Recognize the emotion that you're feeling or, if you can't name the emotion, see if you can determine where you're feeling it.

2. Breathe out. This activates your parasympathetic nervous system and encourages a softening of your mindset.

3. Feel Gratitude. Focus on nature and feel thankful.

4. Re-think, re-position, and re-frame the situation in an encouraging new light.

When you watch athletes competing in sport on TV, you probably notice their routines and behaviours. A great example of this is when Usain Bolt prepares to run his 100-metre sprint. You can see how he actually gets into more of a positive feeling than just a positive mindset. He goes for something that brings positive emotion immediately to him. Positive emotional energy drives peak performance. So, it is super important to Get Your Feelings Right!

You can do all the positive thinking you want, but if your feelings aren't right, and you are consumed by fear or tension, chances are you will not perform your best. I can attest to this first hand as I am learning a new sport: golf! When I bring my awareness to a positive feeling, nine times out of 10 my body does what it's supposed to do, and I can create my best shots. Conversely, when I think about, or am fearful of, a hook into the trees, or a missed hit off the tee, I do exactly that. Where the mind and feelings go, the body follows.

Asserting Your Aggressiveness

Asserting appropriate levels of your own aggressiveness is important to the overall level of power you can generate. This holds true throughout life, not just in sport! When we stand confidently, heart forward, and we project our own powerful energy, we are able to harness more of our inner strength and courage than if we adopt a more passive approach or stance. The message and energy that transmits out of our being is: I'm fully here...and I'm fully ready... Bring it on! It reflects the force of your will. This type of aggressiveness is very firm and confident and it's different from a more irrational type of aggressive energy where we make mistakes in our judgement and slip off the edge of what's reasonable. Athletes find that their best level of energy sits somewhere in the middle of the spectrum and there is a definite zone where we perform at our best. Below is a diagram that describes this optimum level of arousal. It's known as the Yerkes-Dodson Law:

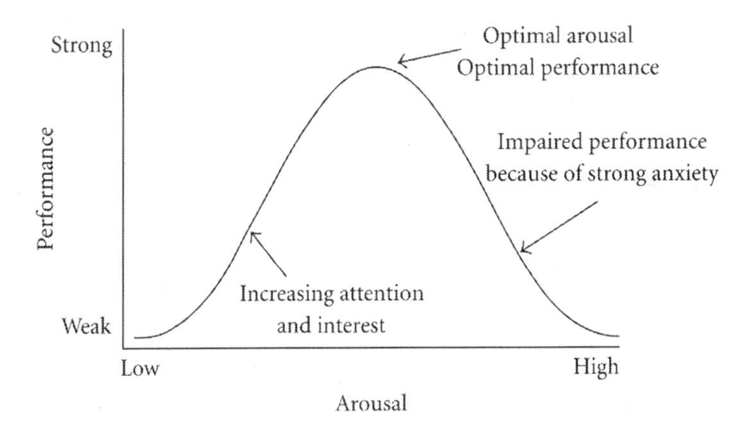

Emotions Affect Performance

Our E-motions, or our "energy in motion" affects our performance. Negative emotions inhibit performance. It's as simple as that and it's true whether you're playing sports or working as an executive in the business world.

- What is your decision-making like when you're angry?
- What is your communication like when you're feeling impatient or frustrated?
- How clear is your focus when you're anxious about something?
- How do you feel at the end of a frustrating and stressful day?

You probably answered "poor" to all four questions. Now, substitute angry, impatient, anxious and frustrating with excited, interested, confident and calm, and the results will be quite the opposite.

Shifting emotion causes approximately 1,400 biochemical changes to take place. Various hormones are secreted in this activity, and cell communication intensifies. Worry, for example, may cause muscle tension; anxiety may upset the stomach. Panic (or any kind of negative emotion) can cause the thinking brain (the cortex) to shut down. Then you can't think clearly: you tighten up and you make mistakes. Cortisol is released and, if we don't put our physiology back in check, then we could be headed for a complete stress meltdown. By contrast, emotions such as appreciation, gratitude and kindness pump dopamine and serotonin through the body, which calms us and helps the thinking brain to function more effectively and efficiently. The result is a more reliable, coherent "best effort."

Practice shifting your energy…Try this:

Shift and Shine: practice feeling positive by calling to mind something that makes you feel good. It might be an experience from the recent past. It might be something inanimate, like a sunset or the stars. It could also be a person or an animal, or a situation you enjoyed. Feel that positive feeling right in your chest area, the area around your heart, and then breathe that feeling in and shine it out from you.

Hard-Wire Your Brain and Cells to Tune into Positivity

When you notice a feeling in your body, you become aware of it. Sometimes our language reflects how our body encapsulates our emotions and holds them in a specific body part—i.e.: "I was so upset when I talked to her that I felt sick to my stomach." Or, "He was a real pain in the neck." Be mindful of your language and how you're describing feelings or emotions in the body. When you are aware of it, you can do something about it: you can choose to shift it, move it or sit with it. When people feel good, they perform better. It is incredibly empowering to realize that you can actually hard-wire your brain to tune into more positivity! Positive emotions act like fuel for the brain and body. On the next page is a diagram that represents two different emotional states and their impact on heart rhythm.

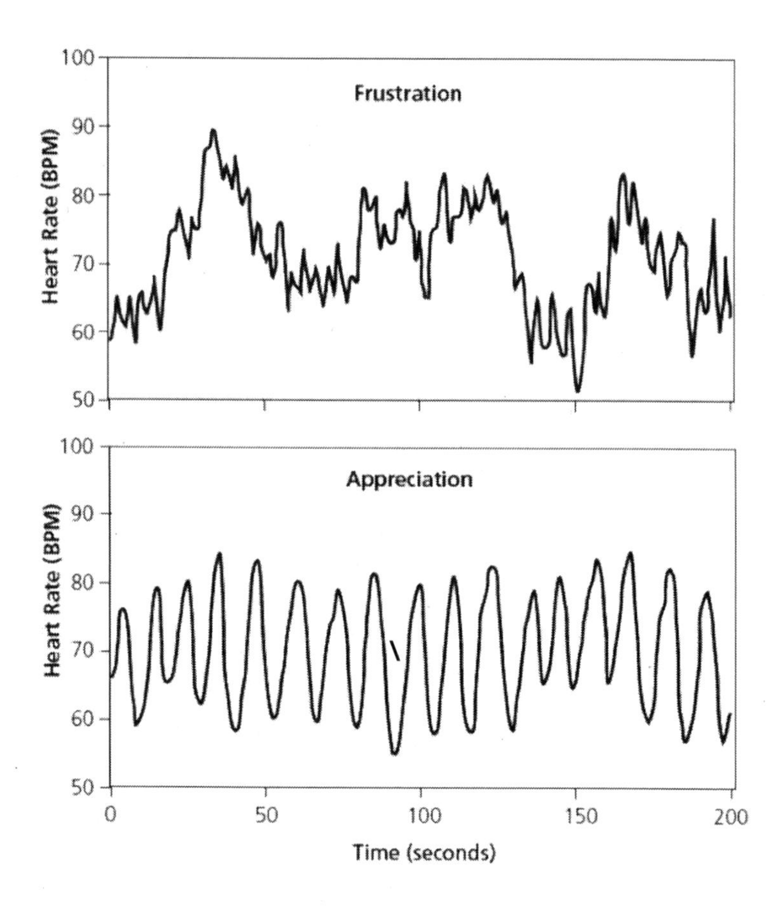

The heart rhythm on top is a trace of heart rate variability that shows an athlete who is feeling anxiety or stress. The trace on the bottom is an example of a regular and rhythmic heart rhythm, when an athlete is in a state of physiological coherence or balance. Positive emotions drive us to create this more rhythmic pattern in our heart rhythms. And this is where we can create our best performances!

That doesn't mean you need to wear a fake smile and pretend that all is well in the world when it really isn't. But you can train yourself to become more aware of what's worth appreciating in your life, and actively seek out people and activities that make you feel better about yourself. Consciously cultivating more positive emotions refuels you, boosts your system, builds resilience and helps you to perform at your best capacity.

Here are five key tips for doing this well:

1. **Express sincere appreciation.** Think about someone on your team for whom you feel appreciation. It may be for a specific action or attribute that you haven't already mentioned to them. Perhaps write a note or send a text message. The person receiving your appreciation will feel good—and you will, too.

2. **Look for things to celebrate.** It might be time to celebrate your own achievements, or those of your teammates. Do you respond positively when someone encourages you, and acknowledges your good work? Recalling and recognizing your achievements builds confidence, too.

3. **Use your "free" words positively.** You have access to an astonishing number of words and every day you get to choose which ones to use and how to use them. Are you maximizing this opportunity? Imagine if a friend stopped by your desk and shared a kind word about a project you are working on. How would that make you feel? A kind word is always appropriate and appreciated. And it affects the giver as well as the recipient.

4. **Recall an experience that generates a positive emotion.** Next time you're about to engage in a task that makes you feel anxious, like public speaking or performing, remember an experience that generates a feeling of confidence and calm. This will keep you from worrying about your mind going blank. The memory doesn't even need to be related to the task at hand, it just needs to generate a positive feeling.

5. **Avoid the "mind–virus" people.** We all know someone who always sees the glass as half empty. These are the folks who can only see the downside of a situation and they complain constantly. These people are energy vampires. You can actually notice after an encounter with such a person that your energy level is lower than it was before you encountered them. They literally suck the positivity and energy out of you, and this can be very toxic. Limit your exposure to such people because emotions are contagious, and negativity is a powerful force that can spread quickly. You are in control of your environment, and you are in control of what you choose to let in to your personal energetic space.

Another aspect of energy relates to your nutritional intake. Imagine that your body is like a sporty racing car and all of the latest research and technology has gone into making it perform at its absolute best. Would it make sense after all of that effort and intention to put substandard fuel into it? When I started paying attention to easy shifts and modifications I could make in my own diet and nutrient intake, I was able to directly affect my performance on the water. This worked for me when I was competing, and it still does today, now that I am a business owner.

Fuel and energy IN = Fuel and energy OUT.

Avoidance Patterns and Energetic Depletion

Throughout my childhood, and for years afterward, I suffered from severe allergies. I had chronic sinusitis, which meant that my body was working extra hard all the time, just to transfer oxygen to my cells. I also had exercise-induced asthma and I was prone to colds and the flu. I spent most of my athletic career feeling afraid of getting sick. I would isolate myself from my teammates because I was afraid they might be sick, and the lack of engagement meant that I got left out of a lot of fun activities. Imagine how alone I felt!

I can't recall exactly when I stopped allowing myself to have fun, but I guarantee you, it was not what I had had in mind for my life. I spent many hours alone in my room watching DVDs and movies or TV shows, and I would only leave to train, eat or get a massage. I didn't realize that this behaviour would have a lingering effect on me for many years. I started to become afraid of being out in public. The effect this had on my being was not positive. I felt depressed, sad and angry at times. It was all my own doing. Worst of all, everything I was doing stopped being fun, too. I was losing my joy, and my spirit, and it was affecting my energy.

Have you ever purposefully isolated yourself or cut yourself off from your friends? If you ever have this feeling, or notice that you're doing this, I encourage you to just do the opposite and take a baby step to re-engage. Reach out or accept an invitation—in person. Being connected online in the virtual world is different from feeling connected with people face-to-face in real time. There is value in live experiences and person-to-person contact. I've spent a lot of my life in front of a screen, partitioning myself off from the world. I encourage you, Beauty: the world needs you and your energy. Be part of it. You never know what experiences that invitation might bring. When you engage with the world, the world engages with you. When you cut yourself off, you deprive yourself of the energy available outside the muffled cocoon of your self.

Show interest and show that you're engaged. I remember the first time I felt part of my team again. It was when I was paddling K4. I deliberately made myself visit with my teammates, even if I was afraid I'd get sick or that I wouldn't be accepted. I started trusting myself around people again, and felt that they valued having me around. Most importantly, I valued them. As I became more comfortable with being part of a larger community, I found that being with people could energize me. It was a powerful lesson.

Seven Steps to Increasing Your Energy

Step 1: Connect with yourself and others every day

- Take 10 seconds to breathe mindfully, at a slow and rhythmic pace. Do this when you first arrive at school or work in the morning, when you take your lunch break, before you go home and before you go to sleep

- Let others be heard. Communicate through engaged listening first. Value someone else's position or view, and then mindfully share your thoughts
- Do something that you enjoy doing every week

Step 2: Move it and shake it!

- Get Up! Stand Up! Just like the song by Bob Marley. Take three minutes every hour to get up, stretch or walk around. This will do wonders for your joint health, pain management and focus!
- Sweat a little every day! Walking, gardening, working out, playing with your little brothers and sisters, or kids if you have them. It all counts. Just move every day.
- Incorporate some flexibility and desk stretches to revitalize your workday and help with pain management and focus.

Step 3: Fuel it!

- We are what we eat. Think mindfully about your food choices and what you will need to do, or work you need to perform.
- Consider making healthy choices 80% of the time! It doesn't have to be perfect. If you give the body the nutrients it needs, you will effectively reduce cravings and perform better!
- Include healthy fats, fibre and protein into your meal and snack choices
- Try smoothies, salads in a jar and quick oats as fast grab-and-go meals or snack ideas

Step 4: Welcome fun and adventure!

- Laughter is really the best medicine AND it is fantastic exercise for the heart and lungs!
- Subscribe to a joke blog or share a funny story with friends or family members
- Include the fun factor in your work, workouts, social time and family time
- Try new things: a new walking trail, board game, activity, restaurant, recipe...

Step 5: Appreciate

- Gratitude is one of the most powerful human emotions
- Keep a gratitude journal or list by your desk or bedside
- Write three-to-five new reasons to be grateful each day and focus on why you feel grateful
- Be sure to include one gratitude statement about YOU everyday

Step 6: Create a supportive environment

- Set yourself up for success by ensuring you have the foods you will need in your fridge and pantry before you need them. Say no to the extras that will not maximize your health and well-being. When you want a treat, go out and get it!
- Clear your workspace to help with focus and productivity
- Arrange a relaxing sleep environment
- Be mindful of electronics and social media, etc., as potential distractions. Set your phone on silent or vibrate and flip it over, or stow it safely away.

Step 7: Allow for time, space and self-care.

- Give yourself some space! Create breathing spaces in your day
- Give the honour of present, engaged attention to another person when you are with them
- Turn off electronics at mealtimes and connect through conversation
- Try body rolling, massage or flotation and meditation for self-care, or simply take an Epsom salts bath to ease stress, joint pain and enhance recovery from whatever ails you

Strong Nutrition

This section of the book is specifically designed to help the new strong beauty navigate the kitchen. Strong nutrition starts with your foundations and your choices. We become what we consume, and the energy we take in is reflected in our outputs and our performances. So, if you want to focus well and do your best work, be sure to start with the basics of a healthy, strong nutrition practice.

My general rule of thumb has always been to eat a variety of foods that are high in nutrients. That includes all of my meals and snacks. I recognized the importance of this when I was competing and felt very quickly if I consumed the wrong foods, I would get upset stomach, or heartburn, or I would feel agitated.

I focus on the big macronutrients: Fat, Fibre and Protein! I choose organic when I can, but I know that it's not always available. My biggest sources of protein are eggs, fish, beef and chicken, and I try and create my own rubs, sauces and salad dressings. Store-bought items are easy, but they are also full of preservatives and sugar, and at times only the cheaper oils. When I create them myself, I know exactly what's in them and the power nutrient substitutions I can make for a bigger impact!

Healthy Hydration 101

How many of you have ever felt that 3:00 p.m. slump of fatigue set in? Did you know that fatigue is often linked to dehydration? Hydration is so important that even if you are only 5% dehydrated, your performance capacity can decline by as much as 30%! In fact, exercise performance is affected even when we are 2% dehydrated! Imagine the impact of dehydration on your work! It is ultra-important to keep our bodies highly hydrated for safety, alertness and job performance, especially in the heat.

What is Healthy Hydration?

Healthy hydration means consuming water instead of sugary beverages and green tea over coffee (coffee is a diuretic). If you do drink coffee, you will need to take in an equal amount of water to offset its impact.

How much water do you need?

- For males: 3-4 litres of water per day
- For females: 2-3 litres of water per day

You'll need more if you're exercising, and more if you're losing a lot of water through sweat.

How does temperature affect hydration?

Work in hot weather means hydration must increase by about 0.5 litre.

How do you drink that amount of water?

Set yourself up for success: try filling a re-usable water bottle at regular intervals during the day. For example, filling your water bottle at 7:00 a.m., 11:00 a.m. and 3:00 p.m. I add slices of lemon or cucumber to my water bottle, or mix it with pure cranberry juice or lemon juice for a full-flavoured boost. When I'm training, I add branched chain amino acids to this mix for a nutrient boost to power my workout and get my recovery started!

Drink UP!

*Strengthen
your roots
and believe
in your growth*

CHAPTER 7: "R" is for Resilience and Responsibility

Our response to situations reflects how we perceive the world. When we experience a situation, our brains interpret and filter information through a structure called the thalamus. It stores our memories and helps filter our new experiences in light of what has happened to us before, thereby generating either positive or negative emotional reactions. So, response is tied, in large part, to memory and experience. It works this way so our brain can shuttle the information to one of two different areas: to the brainstem, which triggers the fight-or-flight, or stress response, or to the cortex, the thinking brain, where rational responses are generated.

Chances are good that sometimes we will react to a perceived threat with a fight-or-flight response even when no threat exists. So, the challenge, then, is to access our thinking brain while we are in a state of stress. If you've read this far, you'll know that I feel it is our responsibility to take care of our own bodies—and how we react to stress is no different. Did you know you can choose to view a situation in whatever way you desire? Focus on what you can control, what is good, the feeling that you want to engage, and the outcome you would like, and you will be golden!

Gratitude

Be Thankful.

- For mentors and role models.
- For moments and experiences.
- For people in our path.

It's super important to be thankful for what you have. Be thankful EVERY DAY for your parents, your friends, your teacher, your lunch, your brother, your sister...your life. Everyone can find many things to be thankful for each and every day. Unfortunately, most people spend too much time complaining, rather than being thankful. Don't be that person.

Did you know that being grateful for all aspects of your life will help you create even more things to be thankful for? By being thankful you are creating a better world for you. This is such an important part of being a successful person. You can start this today. Who can you thank today for helping you be you? Learn to say thank you many times a day to people who help you get closer to your goals. This will make them feel special and important, and it will create a positive vibe in your world.

Thank your parents for driving you to practice, your teacher for helping you with that math question, your brother or sister for cheering you on during your big game…

Shift Your Energy

Kindfulness is the new mindfulness

Plant the seed of loving kindness each day. Start this first thing in the morning. Before your feet hit the floor enjoy a big stretch and take a big breath while still in your bed...generate a feeling of love for your parents or your caregivers. For your teachers and coaches. For your friends and teammates. For your role models and your siblings. Start with this feeling in the centre of your chest and radiate it throughout your whole body like a white light. Now, shift that energy and radiate it out from your heart to someone in your world. Send loving kindness or just warmth. Imagine it emanating from your heart and reaching out into the world. Doing this first thing in the morning will set your day up to have positive encounters. It all starts with one seed, one thought, one action.

Bonus Section

Set Your Week up for Success!

Journalling has many benefits. Use it as a free-flowing form of expression or add as much structure as you like. I use the following framework as a guideline each week and I offer it to you as a tool: this little success habit is a game-changer! I do this religiously each Sunday and look forward to enjoying it along with my cup of coffee! I call it my Sunday Summit.

Karen's Sunday Summit Template

Date: ______________________________

Achievements this week: ______________________________

____

____

Things I made progress on this week: ______________________________

____

____

Challenges/learning this week: ______________________________

____

____

Goals/Intentions to work toward for next week: ______________________________

____

____

Success/Progress next week will mean I have ______________________________

____

____

Thoughts/Realizations: ______________________________

____

____

Interesting connections/Linkages… ______________________________

____

____

Things I leave to the Universe to sort out… ____________________

____

____

Things I release from my energy as they are not within my control… ____

____

____

Strong Health Habits:

1. ____

2. ____

3. ____

Power Check-In, I'm feeling… ____________________

On a scale of 1-10____________________

Word of the week: ____________________

I am grateful for:

1. ____

2. ____

3. ____

WOW Factor! Add in your biggest wow or win of the week.

____

____

The gold lies in the nuggets of learning and growth . . . even if it feels like failure.

CHAPTER 8: Journeying through Adversity

I am...more than medals and muscles. And today, YOU are enough. I am going to let you in on a little secret. You have everything it takes within you to be successful. Your inner champion already exists. You simply need to decide to ignite your flame of determination and let yourself go for it! That next game, that next performance, that next test—you can ace them all once you decide to make it happen. Your attitude and approach determine your altitude, as motivational speaker Zig Ziglar once said.

Always remember that you have the ability to talk yourself into or out of success. You just need some systems in place! The good news is that, because you are committed to learning what it takes to be amazing now, you WILL be successful in many areas of your life as you evolve. It all starts and ends with believing in yourself. Build your belief so big that you have a laser beam focus on where you are going and the process that will get you there.

You can use your end goal as motivation, but it is the process or the system of habits and behaviours you engage every day, the little things, that get you closer to that goal. And don't forget: it's super important to celebrate the little things you do along the way!

Remember to use your journal to celebrate every little moment of success and hard work.

Sometimes in your journey to success you will encounter tough days. Everything won't always go your way. So, what do you do when you hit a speed bump on your road to success? You have two choices. You can take your eye off your goal and let it get you down OR you can choose to take the learning lesson and become stronger. Champions take the lesson.

If you can hold the belief that everything is exactly as it should be in your life, you will always look for what your experiences can teach you. It helps you focus on the positives. I am not saying that the concept of "failing" is easy, it's not. It's natural that on your continuing path to becoming better and stronger there will be times when you will feel down on yourself and perhaps you won't achieve your goals. When this happens, I invite you to simply ask yourself, "What can I learn from this so I can be better next time?" Look for the lesson – I Promise you, it is there. Remember, the gold is in the journey...

Another important aspect of being successful is accepting responsibility. To have great results in your life you must learn to take absolute responsibility. This involves acting in integrity and doing what you say you're going to do. And being accountable for your actions, reactions and outcomes. This can be really hard sometimes. Don't get into the habit of blaming others. When we shift the blame off ourselves, we immediately give our power away. You always have choice and you can always put yourself in a central role or position of power in how your experience of life is unfolding. When a perceptively miserable situation occurs, you have a choice about how you react to it. Be the most positive person you know and look for the learning in everything. Hold kindness and love for yourself throughout the process, like you would do for a close friend or a pet.

It's valuable to learn how to simply Be in your life, and to be OK with whatever emotions arise. If you can do that, and love yourself regardless of what happens, you will take a huge step towards building more confidence and greater self-acceptance. That confidence is what will carry you through when those high-pressure situations arise.

"Procrastination is too high a price to pay for fear of failure. To conquer fear, you have to feel the fear and take action anyway. Forget motivation. Just do it. Act your way into feeling, do not wait for positive emotions to carry you forward."

- John C. Maxwell Failing Forward

"Recognize that you will spend much of your life making mistakes. If you can take action and keep making mistakes, you gain experience."

– John C. Maxwell Failing Forward

Success Tip

When presented with a difficult situation, take a deep breath and tell yourself you are exactly where you are supposed to be. This will allow you to search for the lesson in that situation. Once you are open to receive the learning lesson, new possible paths will be presented to you. The key is to engage a positive feeling.

Challenge is part of what we are here to experience. And you may have heard people say that their challenges helped develop their character. This thinking is so wise. You can think of challenge and adversity as stages on a path up a mountain. There are many different routes to take towards that goal. Some of them will be strewn with difficult experiences, injury, sickness, perhaps a difficult team selection process. Dr. Carol Dweck is one of the leading researchers in the field of motivation and she has written extensively on why people succeed and how to foster success.

Her work offers great insights on the importance of fostering a growth mindset. As you learn to adapt, and grow into some new skills, you gain knowledge that will serve you along the way. My moments of challenge have been difficult to face at times, but when they presented themselves to me, I definitely counted myself "in." Three of my most challenging moments come to mind:

1. My injury and recovery.
2. My separation and divorce.
3. My retirement and transition.

"The important thing in life is not the triumph but the struggle, not to have conquered but to have fought well."

Baron Pierre de Coubertin

May I tell you a little more about each of these situations?

1. My injury and recovery.

The thing about resilience is that we don't know we have it until we've journeyed through a time of challenge or struggle. I love this statement by Baron Pierre de Coubertin, the father of the Olympic movement. In the summer of 2004, I learned that I had sustained an L5-S1 disk hernia. The bad part was that we were three weeks away from the Athens Olympic Games. I was devastated. My K4 crew mates and my coach were all relying on me. I was sitting second in the boat, which is a power position, and I was in an extreme amount of pain. I didn't know what to do. I spoke at length with our team doctor and our therapists to get a strategy in place. I knew I had to shift my focus onto what I could do and move it away from what I couldn't do.

I spent three complete days on bedrest, which was the hardest experience of my career. We were training and carrying out our final preparations for the Games in the south of France. I had to be helped to meals by my teammates. I felt vulnerable for the first time in my career. But my teammates stepped up and helped me get back to me. I recall Dr. Don saying to me that I had to take some anti-inflammatory medicines and that perhaps we would consider a nerve block, which sounded scary to me. I knew that if we could control the inflammation, I could handle the pain. I also had to be incredibly careful that I wasn't taking any medicinal substances that were banned or prohibited as performance enhancers. For an athlete who always abides by fair, clean sport, this is paramount. I called up a fellow Olympian, Marnie McBean, who is an Olympic champion in the sport of rowing. She had sustained a similar injury to mine, and had been recovering during the Sydney Olympics, four years earlier. I had met Marnie at those games and we had stayed in contact. She later served as a mentor to me through the Athens and Beijing Olympic Games. I will never forget her advice to me: She told me that I had to:

- Get a good doctor onside—check! Dr. Don MacKenzie was the best in the business!

- I had to rest completely and let the pain and inflammation settle down—basically let the medications start to do their job. And
- I had to repeat over and over to myself: "I'm going to be on that start line!"

I followed her advice as though it were scripture and, sure enough, after a few days, the pain started to subside. Little did I know then that it was going to take about a year-and-a-half until I was actually fully healed. I got to that start line strong and healthy, thanks to the support of my teammates and support system.

My lesson in sharing this little story is to reassure you that, whatever challenge you're facing, find some good, reliable people who have your best interests at heart, and focus on the things that you can control, rather than the immense number of things that are crappy or that you cannot control. Get some good advice and weigh all your options, and then come up with a plan of attack. Even the challenges are part of the journey, and they can be some of our greatest teachers. Focus on the "controllables" and keep fostering that positive environment and mindset. The body has an amazing and awesome ability to heal itself!

Here are some questions I invite you to answer:

Describe a time in your life, recent or past where you did not reach the goal that you set for yourself.

- What did you do to refocus?
- What were the things that you chose to focus on to move you forward?

- Who were the people that helped you to feel better?
- How did you help yourself experience fulfillment?
- What did you do to move from negative thinking/feeling to a more positive outlook?
- What did you learn in the lesson or journey that you have taken forward with you?

As I mentioned earlier, overcoming injury was one of the most trying and difficult experiences of my life. I was in physical pain and my physical capabilities were limited. I was still competing professionally in kayaking, and I was concerned that my healing was not happening fast enough. As with many things in life, healing takes time. You might have to deal with the most traumatic injuries for months, or even years. During that healing time, I became impatient and frustrated and, with that energy, I discovered that I was healing even more slowly.

I didn't make breakthroughs in my healing until I focused on what I could do, rather than what I could not do. I knew without a doubt that, following my disk hernias, my core, as well as the supporting muscles, would be stronger than ever. I looked into alternative methods of training, such as Pilates, yoga and meditation. I optimized my diet and nutritional intake, and I started learning about supplements that would support my healing, as well as therapies.

2. My separation and divorce.

This was tough for me to experience and some days were rougher than others, but the experience taught me the importance of mental health. I am proud of how my ex-husband and I navigated our divorce: throughout the process we maintained our communication, knowing that we wanted to part ways while maintaining a level of mutual respect. Jeremy and I had been together for eight years altogether, seven of them as a married couple, and we were no longer supporting each other's growth. We were fighting a lot, and we both agreed that it was not serving either of us to remain together. To this day, we remain in each other's lives and we are supportive friends from afar. I value that relationship, and I'm glad Jeremy is still in my life.

My separation and divorce came at a tumultuous time in my life. I had not qualified for the London Olympic team and this is what had triggered my decision to retire from sport along with another flare up of my back injuries. The retirement already represented a massive transition for me. I was also taking over the running of the company that Jeremy and I had founded together. I was trying to hold the façade of I Promise Performance together when, in actual fact, everything I had built was crumbling beneath my feet. There were days when I would just cry.

In my journey through divorce, I slowly started to feel that I could finally just be me. I no longer had to put someone else first. In fact, what I learned was that it was very important to start putting myself first again. I found solace in writing and reading, as well as in spending time with friends. I did engage in therapy with a counsellor, and I found that helpful and reassuring. The extra-tough times came when a bad day moved me to start asking difficult questions: Did I make the wrong decision? What did I want my life to feel like? At night I would often text to check in with Jeremy and I would feel sad. The healing of hearts and emotions takes time, more than the healing of our physical being, it seems to me. And although our divorce meant the end of our relationship as it was, it offered a new beginning for both of us.

During my darkest times, I longed for a sense of normalcy. I relied on my structure and my health habits to get me through. My morning run would let me feel like I could breathe and relax into my day, and I would feel strong after an afternoon or evening at the gym. Connecting with my spirit in the yoga room was great for me, too. These were all healthy practices. They were also crutches and vices. I often stayed up late at night, going out for dinner or drinks with friends, and I was literally burning the candle at both ends. I had zero energy and I was hurting myself through excessive exercise. It took me many years to realize I was using exercise as an escape, and today I am very mindful of that tendency. At the time, however, I experienced a recurrence of old injuries because I was igniting old patterns and old beliefs. I even sustained a second disk hernia, which bound me to my bed, and required a lot of chiropractic care. For nearly a month I was only able to work standing up. I had to get very painful injections into my back as nerve blocks (an epidural injection) as well as injections into the bursas of my hip. I now enjoy exercise and movement every day, but I do not need it at all costs in order to function fully. I now listen to the wisdom in my body and mind, as well as my energy, before I go out to mindlessly train. I also make time for self-care, which I will discuss in a later chapter.

3. My transition and retirement.

Making the decision to retire came pretty quickly for me. I recall being in Atlanta at the Olympic trials in the spring of 2012 (the fifth and final set of Olympic trials of my career). I had put a relatively strong week of race preparation behind me, and I felt good heading into my races. But when I reached the 500-metre final, I simply had no gas. I felt like I had failed again, but I knew deep down that this would be my last race. On the dock following the final, I tearfully hugged each of my competitors, and thanked them for the race. I'm sure they thought I was being a bit dramatic, but I was genuinely grateful. It was over. I knew it. There was no coming back. I was weary. I had fended off and healed from many injuries. It was time to hang up my paddle.

I had journeyed back to full form following one long break from competition, and I was proud of the work I had done. I remember leaving the race course that day feeling that I had had a full career. I paddled for the remainder of the summer purely for fun, and I entered some races at the national club competitions that were held on Lake Banook in Nova Scotia. I was proud to be part of all that, but I also knew that I wanted a full break from kayaking. I no longer wished to compete. I raced my final race, packed up my bag and headed home. I accepted a retirement plaque from our association. It was a nice ceremony and I was proud to have my career end where all the racing started in my career, on Lake Banook. I did not have a party. I wasn't in the mood.

I immersed myself in work and training, still maintaining a similar schedule just without the sport itself. It took me about a year to be able to say the words, "I'm retired," and over time that sentence became so much easier. I now say, "I retired five years ago." I love the words of congratulations that I hear from time to time and I am honoured that people recall my time on the water.

The water, waves and wind shaped who I am. Taking daily strokes shaped who I am. The experience and process of your unique journey will also shape who you become. I appreciate my water journey every day. I have made peace with it, as well as my path, and I know that the lake is always there. I often enjoy going for a leisurely paddle or a stand-up paddle on the lake, but it is not part of my day-to-day life. I miss parts of my old life. The friendships, the accountability, being coached, and making daily improvements—they were all gratifying. Being focused on a single subject is also very addictive and satisfying. I now enjoy golf and rock climbing, as well as trail running and skiing, sports that I could not do as freely when I was competing.

Finding a New Path

I often get the opportunity through the Nova Scotia Sport Hall of Fame to speak with kids, and in my message to young people, I am sure to remind them to create multiple outlets for their passions, other hobbies and dreams. The athlete's life is great. I would not trade it for any experience. However, it is finite, and it ends, just as everything does, according to its own cycle. Purposefully pursuing another path is helpful, not only in the process of transition, but for your mental and physical health, as well. My passion is speaking and connecting with others, and I make certain that I am doing enough of that to keep me fuelled and charged. This energy helps me navigate the difficult and challenging times of entrepreneurship.

Celebrate the Little Wins. Every Single One.

Decide early on in your day what your little win and big win will be. What is it that you want to achieve, or how do you want to feel?

I have created a worksheet to help you with this:

STRONG Beauty: Situation Creation Tool

Before any event, test, project, performance, tournament or even through your day, take a moment to get clear about these three things by writing in the space provided.

Situation: ____

Date: ____

Who do you want to BE?

Let's face it… Performing is hard work. We want to be able to do it consistently well. None of us wants to wimp out or be unable to deliver our best. Choose to CREATE your performance rather than REACT to it. Envision WHO YOU WANT TO BE in the situation, i.e.: "I want to be an athlete who is sure of herself."

____

____

____

____

____

____

____

How do you want to FEEL?

Setting the intention for a positive feeling is a huge step. When you tell yourself how you want to feel, you begin to teach yourself that YOU can generate your feelings. Feelings no longer have to happen to you.

___

___

___

___

___

___

___

What is your desired outcome/destination?

Be your own internal GPS system. Know in advance what your best-case scenario will be. Intentionally create your outcome…

___

___

___

___

___

___

___

For your copy of the Situation Creation tool, download it from my site at strongbeauty.ca

My acronym for this is: **WIN**, for **W**hat's **I**mportant **N**ow. When I feel overwhelmed or anxious about something that is coming up I find using this acronym helps to clear my mind of unproductive chatter and it helps me get back to a powerful feeling of presence. I usually whiteboard all of my tasks and to-dos, and then I colour code them into groups. In terms of my business I have categories such as: Fast Cash (high value, high impact), Business Building (Long term growth), Deliverables (Agreed-upon "Have-Tos"), Time Wasters (non-active). I then determine which are the most important and actionable pieces that I can move forward with in order to create some momentum in different areas of my business growth. Try this technique next time, and focus on your own WIN.

Be-Do-Have Versus Do-Have-Be: Moving from Practice to Present Performance.

I love this mantra. Sometimes when I get stuck in my head—or in my list of to-dos—I find it to be helpful, as well. It's especially important for me when I'm preparing for a big event or conference workshop that requires me to be totally engaged and present for my participants. After all the preparation has been done, I let that piece go, and I trust that my body, mind and awareness will know what to do. I still actively get myself ready and engaged to be at my best, but I can actually trust the process now. I go with the flow. That took me a while. When I trust in my process and let experience take over, I am better able to be present and engaged. All the preparation in the world doesn't mean a thing if you aren't able to get yourself to show up and perform. This is the biggest trick, and one that I encourage you to try.

How to do it

Once all the prep work has been done, shift your focus away from all the things you still have to do and, instead, focus on who you will BE. Let your behaviour and actions arise out of this Being energy. It involves being totally engaged, completely present, and breathing fully in calm, clear confidence. This energy and awareness will get you where you need to be to perform at your best.

Stand strong.
Breathe bravery.
Give gratitude.

CHAPTER 9: Resilient Strong Beauty

I truly believe that I am who I am because of my journey and the lessons I have encountered along my path so far. I am ever changing and evolving, and growing, as are you! The toughest moments in my life have led to the greatest awakenings, and I know they have also contributed in large part to my resilience. Getting through the misery of my lower back disk hernias, navigating my divorce, and transitioning out of a career as a professional athlete have been the toughest moments in my life to date.

Being resilient is a skill. Much like riding a bike. You feel wobbly at first, and then, as you become immersed in the situation and its teachings, you gather courage, confidence and strength, and you bounce back. Imagine that resilience is like a tree in the wind. If the tree was rigid, and could not sway and adapt to wind conditions, or move its branches and foliage to distribute energy, it would crack and fall to the ground. Resilience is a flexibility skill and it gives us strength in tough situations. It comes from surviving the mighty winds and staying on course. The key lies in recognizing our energy, and the level at which we are performing, so we can determine how we need to be, in order to shift our chosen actions and behaviours, if necessary. It's important to remember that all emotions are valid, and they are all a manifestation of energy. We all experience a plethora of emotions every day, and many of us are getting good at labelling them (partly due to emoticons, I believe!). But sometimes, it is OK to just be with an emotion, and let it ride itself out, like a wave. With time, and conscious breathing, it will move along, as all energy does. Being present is one way that we can become more resilient. I've included more resilience skillsets later in this book, and I hope that they are as useful to you as they have been for me.

The skill in this area relates to how we can prepare ourselves, proactively, to better handle situations in life. I'm a huge believer in the importance of preparation as well as the value of acquiring skills and knowledge.

The Hurricanes of Life

Remember that the winds and waves of life will blow and swell, and it is your job to find your balance, navigate and keep driving forward. It is through these struggles and bad weather that we gain strength and learn about our resilience and our core being. The gold is in the journey, and I Promise you it's there, discoverable, if you're willing to do the work to mine for it.

Relaxation is Power

"One minute to start...please approach the start line." This was the familiar voice of our chief starter and official at the World Championships

The boats move into the start boots (like blocks in track and field) and are set in position. As I move the nose of the boat to rest gently, but firmly on the front of the boot, I feel alive and ready. My heart is pumping through my chest, my palms are sweating, and it feels like the competitors, collectively, represent a stable of race horses before the bell at the Kentucky Derby. Maybe that's why I enjoy watching horse racing: it's all about the anticipation of the race, the breathing, and that moment before everything begins.

I smell sweat and carbon fibre and the water, as well as the possibility of personal success. And yet there is a strong, still silence hanging in the air in anticipation of the gun.

"Start within 10 seconds...!"

I love that moment. It gives me quiet comfort. My sport psychologist told me years after I stopped competing that not many people love that moment. But it was the moment where I felt most alive and full of potential. Perhaps that's why I love public speaking so much. All the preparations are complete, and everyone is ready to perform. When I was competing, what lay ahead were 100 perfect strokes over 200-metres, and they had to be strong and solid to propel my boat forward with powerful precision and ease.

My breath is steady, and I tell myself to breathe OUT, OUT, OUT. This is my cue to let my shoulders sink into their strongest posture. That small cue is enough to signal an automatic chain of commands that ready me for performance. Explosive power. That is the key. Strong and solid rotations to the core power my strokes and strong shoulders to hold up the world. The skill to be resilient in this moment takes years of work and purposeful, intentional practice; the goal is to gain confidence in every situation, to be prepared for the moment of the start, and the ensuing race, however it is presented.

Relaxation equates to power and speed, whereas tension limits our power and sense of ease. It is the same in life, in my experience so far.

Mastery through Resilience

What makes someone a master of anything? Skateboarding, sinking a free throw, martial arts, public speaking, creating beautiful works of art, programming, playing beautiful music or solving problems...they all require skill developed through persistent practice, and the ability to relax in the moment. Researchers say it takes 10,000 hours of practice to become masterful at any one skill.

While training in my sport of sprint kayaking, I learned that by forcing my efforts too much, my mind and my muscles actually generated less power. If I were too tense, and tried too hard during a race, I could not effectively transfer power into the water, and the boat would not move as fast. If I relaxed in the moment and leveraged my breath, the power in my strokes increased dramatically.

Yoga and meditation are two examples of practices where we learn to use our mind and body to maximize our flexibility and our ability to relax during challenging times. This is incredible for the mind: it helps build resilience. My coach used to tell me to "try easy" and my mantra was "Trust" and "Smile." When I work with Olympians, high-level athletes, and business executives who are in high-pressure situations, I ask them to breathe and soften areas where their bodies are tense; when the body relaxes, the mind follows. This skill can be applied to anything we do to increase the impact of what we do. Here are some ideas for moving into that relaxation space:

1. Surround yourself with positive and encouraging people.

The people you surround yourself with become part of your energy. Being mindful of who we spend time with can help give us energy, or take away from it. Have you ever felt drained of energy, or more negative, from talking to a particular person? If so, ask yourself if this relationship is continuing to serve you, and if it supports you in your goals. If the answer is no, then perhaps try to spend a little less time with that particular person and take note of any change in energy and experience that result. Notice, too, when you are around people whose presence uplifts you and fills you with hope and promise. Most of the time, a positive interaction is more helpful than a negative one. I Promise, the people we surround ourselves with and spend energy with make a difference to our quality of life. Check in and be sure that you are honouring yourself and your values in your relationships with others, as well as in the relationship you have with yourself.

"We do not need magic to transform the world. We carry all the power we need inside ourselves already."

– J.K. Rowling

2. Be willing to learn: be a student of the game and of life.

To be in a state of continuous learning requires adopting a "growth mindset" instead of a fixed mindset. When we are growing, we are pliable and flexible, and open to new opportunities. When we are in a fixed mindset, we stagnate and become comfortable with a static pattern; we accept the status quo. To break outside of the barriers that you come across, try to view challenges as lessons in the moments of life; they are part of your journey. When you come up against a barrier, explore it and seek to learn from it, and then trust your skills and experience to just keep you travelling on through!

In the summer of 2016, I got to be part of the CBC broadcast team at the Rio Olympic Games, fulfilling the role of colour commentary for canoe-kayak. It was a highlight experience for me but I had a lot to learn. I knew I wanted to do some broadcast work after my first live experience in the booth at a sprint cup race in Toronto. I was instantly hooked to the energy in the broadcast trailer and I was thrilled that the camera people and producers were looking to me as the expert. I felt such a part of the team in Rio with CBC and prior to the Olympic Games. I got to participate in a lot of live shows of Road to the Olympic Games, with host Scott Russell and commentator, Brenda Irving. The minute I entered the CBC building in downtown Toronto, I had a moment of sheer excitement followed by sheer terror. They trusted in me and my abilities and I had never done anything of this magnitude. I guess in their mind, I had already competed on the world stage and done many interviews. Being willing to learn and grow is the key to becoming resilient. Knowing that you are not by any means perfect and you're not expected to be.

The experience of being a student continually immersed in learning was addictive to me. CBC provided me with coaching, feedback, and tremendous mentors and role models in the lead-up to the Olympics. It was an experience I will never forget and for which I am so grateful. I heard Ron Maclean's voice over the headset and the countdown to "We're LIVE in 3…2…1…" in my ear. The Olympic music played in the background and the Christ the Redeemer (the Christo) statue watched over my head as I looked out over the Olympic waters, taking it all in. It was a moment of heartfelt excitement, passion and connectedness and I was so ready and IN, and invested in sharing the stories of the athletes and their journey with the world.

Lessons and opportunities to learn and grow come your way every day that can help you be a better version of you. I challenge you to search those opportunities out and when they're presented or offered to you, run at them with an open mind to learn as much as you can. And don't forget to savour the moment, take it all in and feel that strength as you smile.

3. Be an optimist!

Be the most positive person you know. We are more resilient when we are optimistic.

BELIEVE IN YOU. ALWAYS. Build positive belief so big that you begin to create and become what you envision. It's the little things in your life that lead to the big things. Say to yourself, "I AM creating the best version of the highest vision of me." What does the best version of you look like?

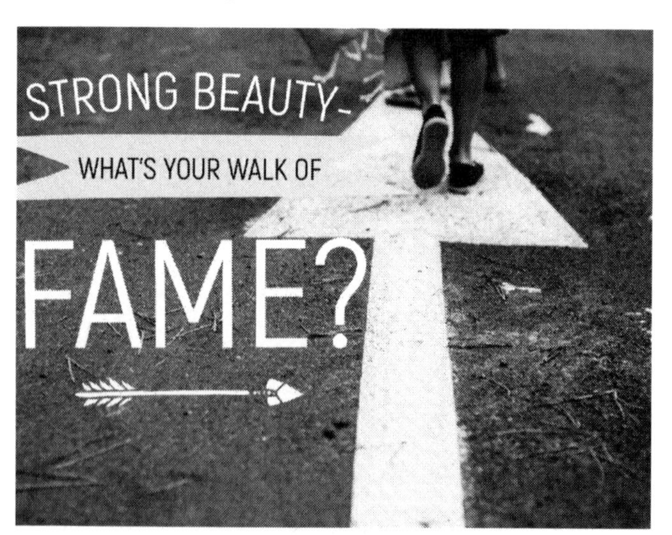

Photo by Nadia Jamnik on Unsplash

The "I AM" mantra...

I encourage you to take five minutes each day and introduce a powerful practice into your life. It involves pairing a specific method of breathing with mantras that will help you focus on what you wish to create in your life. You want to be thankful for your breath every day. It gives you life, energy, power and focus. You can use that breath to focus on what you really want in life.

I find mantras helpful to me as well, especially now that I am no longer an elite athlete who receives coaching every day. I am an #entrepreneurathlete and I must generate my own energy from one day to the next. The same challenges come up for me as an entrepreneur as when I was an athlete. Confidence and delivering service are chief among them. I have always focused on the question of what value I bring to the table and I've worked hard to get clear on the answers. I centre myself and prepare solidly for meetings, phone calls, presentations and pitches. That is all part of my process. How I choose to walk through this world is an important part of how I show up with clients. It is not a "sometimes" thing. It is an "all the time" thing. Just like competing. You show up every day and practice the way you want to perform in the final competition. It's that simple. There are no short cuts.

Let's practice the "I AM" mantras:

Take a deep breath and think "I AM" as you exhale I want you to focus on what you want to feel and bring into your life.

I AM...Strong

I AM...Peaceful

I AM...Present

I AM...Kind

I AM...Smart and eager for more knowledge

I AM...Inspired

I AM...Helpful

I AM...Amazing

I AM...Successful

I AM...a Winner

I AM...IN!

I AM...Tough

I AM...Beautiful

The words I AM create the feeling that you are in the moment already. It's powerful stuff...Give it a try!

What you choose to do when no one else is watching is what separates a champion from everyone else.

Adapted from a John Wooden quote

CONCLUDING Thoughts

Strong Transformation

As an Olympic kayaker for nearly 20 years, my transition out of competitive sport was an emotional experience, even though I was ready for it. My hope is that by reading this book and engaging in some of the exercises and practices it offers, you will find your own journey to be a little easier. Transition—whether it involves a sport, a new school, a new phase of life or career—can feel messy. When I was racing, I always found the transition phase of the race the most challenging to manage. The transition in kayak racing happens after the start, when your energy systems shift from burning predominantly carbohydrate for fuel and energy to burning more fat. It is the most uncomfortable feeling in the world to overcome. I was afraid of it for years until I learned to be gentler with myself and my experience. Your muscles literally feel all tied up with lactic acid and other by-products of intense exercise and you must push through that confidently and intentionally to reach your race speed. This is also the time that you must remain disciplined in your mind and your language of support to yourself.

When you eventually get into your rhythm and groove in the race, it never feels easy. That wall always comes, even with the best training and preparation. Being willing to feel uncomfortable, and staying confident — even when I felt fear and intense pain — helped me. My confidence came from my committed practice and it helped me manage the transition phase of the race. What I learned through my years on the water is that if you can remain positive, and committed to the journey—even through the pain and challenge—you can emerge into new levels of your greatness. It is the same with any transition in life. There are pain points, times when you will feel downright uncomfortable; walls come up in front of you every day.

I challenge you to consider exploring genuine commitment to you, and invest in your process. Love yourself through the process, no matter what it brings to you. When you notice yourself feeling defeated, or you hear that negative voice in your head that speaks up at challenging times and tells you why you can't do something, remember that YOU CAN, and YOU ARE IN. You are strong, Beauty!

Thank you so much for reading this book and engaging with the exercises within it. Strong Beauty is all about having deep respect for you and your process and providing helpful tools along the way to light your path. I want to honour and send deep gratitude to you for reading these words and I ask you to please consider spreading the word of #strongbeauty among your peers and family members. Remember, with presence and committed, strong work, there is no limit to what you can achieve along your journey. Make sure to have fun along the way!

See the beauty within you and also in others. I wish you the best of success in your journey.

With loving kindness, Karen and Promise.

If you'd like to stay connected to our Strong Beauty tribe, please consider following us on social media: Instagram- @strongbeautytribe.

Sign up at strongbeauty.ca to get free resources and find out about the *Strong Beauty CORE* retreat days near you.

I leave you with these words:

SHE is beautiful, but not like the photoshopped women in magazines.

She is beautiful, for the way she thinks and loves.

She is beautiful, for the sparkle in her eyes when she talks about something she loves.

She is beautiful, for her ability to make other people smile, even if she is sad.

No, she isn't beautiful for something as temporary as her looks. She is beautiful, deep down to her soul.

She IS beautiful as a Being …
and that is how I see her.

Adapted quote from Wild Woman Sisterhood

TOOLS and Appendices

Appendix A

Healthy hydration is important! Here is a great alternative to water when you want to spice up your daily drink! This recipe is also a great energy booster:

1 litre of water or green tea

1 tbsp. maple syrup or honey

1 tbsp. lemon juice or pure, unsweetened cranberry juice

Pinch of sea salt

Optional: Frozen blueberries

Appendix B

Green Monster Smoothie!

Do you ever feel you need super human strength? Well, I do!

I am sharing my go-to power smoothie for fast fuel and nutrient power that will last all day!

Ingredients:

A massive handful of spinach

A dollop of plain Greek yogurt

A squeeze of honey

1 whole banana (frozen or not)

1 tbsp chia seeds

1 tbsp flax seeds

A dollop of Coconut oil or MCT oil

1 tsp Chlorella (superfood algae and it increases "good" bacteria in the gut)

1 scoop of Bulletproof Hydrolyzed collagen powder

2 tbsp peanut butter

Unsweetened vanilla almond milk

Vanilla protein powder

Puree ingredients and drink throughout your morning or recovery day!

Appendix C

Fuelling on the Fly

As many of you know, summer can be BUSY! Most of us are on the go traveling, camping, visiting family, participating in or watching sporting events, or just generally juggling life's tasks. Healthy eating can be hard when we are so busy.

Here are my favorite tips for fuelling on the fly!

Pack your snack.

Airports are often stacked with high-priced, low-value foods. Your snacks need to be easy to carry and consume on-the-run. Home-made trail mix, pulses and pre-cut veggies—even hard-boiled eggs—make good, portable choices and can be easily eaten in the airport or on the go.

Scope out the local fare.

Search for fibre-rich foods and good quality sources of protein. As a general rule, healthy fat, fibre and protein should be components of all snacks and meals.

Bottle your water.

Carrying a re-usable water bottle that you can refill will help you to go the distance of your journey. Be sure to hydrate regularly to help things move smoothly.

Re-think your drink.

Power your drink with non-sugar supplements for an additional boost. Vitamin C or magnesium powder sachets offer a great way to add powerful vitamins and minerals to your drink. Adding natural sweeteners instead of sugar-laden options will keep you feeling refreshed and fully hydrated. Try honey, green tea, lemon juice or cranberry juice to add flavour and some extra electrolytes.

Meal-Boosters.

Try carrying small, travel-size sachets of: Chia seeds, coconut butter, nut butters and hemp seeds that you can add to meals. Energy bars, protein powders and greens are also great meal supplements to ensure that you have high performing nutrition on the road.

Appendix D

Easy-peasy super saucy sauce!

INGREDIENTS:

1 large can crushed tomatoes

1 onion

3 celery hearts

2 cloves garlic

2 peppers

Veggies- carrots, zucchini, yellow squash, mushrooms

Meat—choice of: Italian sausage, ground turkey, ground pork, ground beef

Brown rice noodles

DIRECTIONS:

Sauté onion and meat together in a large iron pot on the stove on medium heat.

Once meat is fully cooked, add in the veggies that need more cook time (i.e.: carrots).

Add in other veggies and the sauce, then simmer on low heat for one hour.

Cook pasta as per package directions and drain

Serve together with crusty bread and enjoy!

Reserve leftover sauce and freeze for future meals

MEAL PLANNING FOR THE WIN!

Batch cooking has always offered the best support for my week. I find this especially helpful when I'm feeling tired and not knowing what to prepare. I can batch cook sauces and stews and freeze them for future meals. I also prepare salads and my own salad dressings that I can use as meals or supports throughout my week. I enjoy the process of cooking my own food, and I always have.

You might also take advantage of a meal kit delivery service, too.

One of my favorites is Hello Fresh! I believe Hello Fresh! is offered in major cities around the world. My meals come once per week. The ingredients and sauces are pre-measured and ready for me to cook. All the recipes are laid out for me. In my experience so far, this takes the challenge of the grocery shop and the planning of meals out of the equation. I can eat a variety of foods every week and I have plenty of leftovers for other meals. I have very little food waste, which used to be a problem for me. I highly recommend this option for people who are starting out with preparing meals or for those who just want the planning, shopping and delivery done for them. It would also be useful for students as well as young busy working professionals. I wish this had been available when I was at training camp—it would have saved me energy.

Appendix E

Items for the Grocery Store Guru

I always shop in the organic section of the grocery store because it is much smaller and easier to navigate than all those aisles! Here are my go-to staples for my kitchen and pantry!

GROCERY:
Coconut oil
Garlic
Ginger
Rice Pasta
Tomato soup
Canned crushed tomatoes
Canned chick peas
Vegetable broth
Chicken broth
Canned tuna
Canned salmon
Various nuts and seeds
Dark chocolate
Spices (paprika, cayenne, ginger, turmeric, oregano, steak spice
Whole grain crackers
Apple sauce
Olive oil
Risotto (boxed)
Sauerkraut
Chia seeds
Energy bars (low glycemic)

DAIRY:
Cheeses
Eggs
Almond or cashew milk
Full fat Greek-style yogurt
Kefir

MEATS:
Ground beef, turkey or lamb
Beef steaks
Chicken thighs
Beef jerky

PRODUCE:
Fruit: berries, apples and oranges and anything in-season, lemons, limes
Veggies: spinach, broccoli, peppers, mushrooms, onions

STRONG SUPPLEMENTS AND NUTRIENT SUPPORT:
High quality Protein powder
Collagen powder (if high volume or high impact sport)
Branched chain amino acids (if high intensity training)
Vitamin C
Probiotics
Vitamin B
Vitamin D
High quality fish oil (omega 3)
Minerals (calcium, magnesium, zinc)

Appendix F

Highlight Reel

Create your own Highlight Journal…

Draw or write the good things or feelings that you experienced today…

Please visit strongbeauty.ca to download your Strong Beauty C.O.R.E (Care, Openness, Resilience and Energy) program tool box pages.

Appendix G

Strong Mindset

The Strong Beauty C.O.R.E. Program was created to teach young women the core principles of having a strong mindset. The acronym stands for Care, Openness, Resilience and Energy. In my work with the Nova Scotia Sport Hall of Fame, I get to travel around Nova Scotia. I am often asked what made me a success, given that I came from such a small town. I believe that it was because of my mindset. I made up my mind to achieve my goal and I was determined to make it happen. In fact, I saw it happen before it ever actually did. So, in that way, I created it myself, just as you can.

I believe strongly in my work through Strong Beauty and recognize the need to teach young women the skill sets required for success in life. I have created the C.O.R.E. program to teach around the areas of health, movement, nutrition, mindset and financial wellbeing. My vision is to expand these programs throughout the Atlantic provinces to help young women manage difficult times of transition.

Appendix H

Strong Movement

Part of my passion for creating my program, Strong Beauty, has been to help girls develop a positive relationship with healthy physical activity.

I start with **Strong Core** because I believe girls need to identify and act from their core values. Strong Core Strength helps them focus on their values and create a positive outlook on exercise.

Strong Legs are important to build the foundation that allows us to stand and show up in the world. Leg strength is about balance, agility and support. We need strong legs not only for power in sport, but also in life.

Strong Backs are important to provide backup for ourselves—and each other, to be accountable to one another and BE who we say we are going to be. Strong Backs are as important in the boardroom as on the podium and in front of a class. When we take on risks and know that we are backed and supported, we can go forward with confidence to inspire new strengths.

Strong Shoulders are important because of the work we do in the world. Sometimes we shoulder the burdens of a world in pain, and that world relies on us. We need strong shoulders to carry that opportunity to serve. We lift each other up.

Strong Lungs and Hearts are important because we need the fitness capability to move our best selves forward to serve and help others in the world. When we show up strong and fit, we can handle the world with care and compassion.

Strong Minds are important because we want to have the mental strength and stamina necessary for connecting with ourselves and those we serve. Meditation and mindfulness facilitate this strong mind, and it is always a work in progress.

I have included a Strong Workout for you to try!

21-15-9 WORKOUT

Complete 21 reps of each exercise, followed by 15 reps of each exercise, and finally 9 reps of each exercise. Drink water and take breaks as needed.

Strong Self-Care

Strong Self Care is the biggest key of all in this journey to creating Strong Resilience. It is the one thing that truly makes the biggest difference. If you're working hard and serving people, it is tough to feel replenished without a regular self-care routine. Whether you're a top athlete or a community volunteer, we all need some tender loving self-care on a regular basis. When we care for ourselves, we are more able to fully care for others. This is not a pursuit for Sundays alone, but I love to pay extra special attention to myself on Sundays! The biggest breakthrough is to realize that self-care is not selfish: Self-Care is a success strategy!

This piece has made far and away the biggest impact on my performance as an athlete, a speaker, and a business person. Funnily enough, I paid tons of attention to it while I was competing, and completely ignored it as an unnecessary and expensive "extra" after I retired from Olympic competition. I began spending my time helping others develop positive health habits, and I started travelling a lot to speak at conferences and deliver workshops. I always maintained my workouts and my solid nutritional practices and sleep habits, but self-care was left by the wayside. My body started screaming at me to fix that oversight! In the summer of 2016, I was experiencing so much physical pain in my lower back and hips that I had to take notice. And then I discovered "floating." My first experience with Flotation Therapy was a bit scary. After all, it requires you to float in a warm tank in total darkness and you can choose complete sensory deprivation if you choose to close the hatch! Prior to trying it, I had read of the enormous benefits that floating can bring. Epsom salts, magnesium, meditation, mindfulness and warm water bathing—many of my favorite things—all combine to bring the participant an extraordinary experience that supports health and well-being. For me, floating is extremely efficient as well. All I do is show up, strip off my clothes and lie down to float in the water. Whatever comes up for me flows through me and passes into the warm waters. It is a very sacred and special time for me and I highly recommend it. It is a blissful chance to love and care for myself. I know I show up as a better person in all areas of my life when I follow this practice.

Appendix I

Other Ideas for Looking After Yourself:

Bathe in Epsom Salts

There are many benefits to bathing in Epsom salts. First and foremost is the relaxation that comes from gently soaking in warm water. This is very healing for joints and tissues, and also for muscular recovery and the removal of lactic acid. Epsom salts are high in magnesium, which is a mineral that is easily absorbed by the skin, our largest and most exposed organ! When we absorb magnesium into our body, we experience an immediate calming effect, which helps with managing stress. One of the effects of having an increased intake of magnesium is a deeper, more restorative sleep.

Body Rolling

Body rolling or "foam rolling" is becoming more and more common. You might have seen foam rollers used for tissue rolling at gyms—they have various shapes and sizes, as well as varying levels of density. The key to foam rolling is to make the time to do it. There are tremendous health benefits, such as decreased tissue tension and decreased risk for injury. The practice can be used in conjunction with warm-up exercises to raise the temperature and pliability of muscles and supporting tissues. It helps manage the body's waste materials, such as lactic acid, and thereby facilitate a faster recovery. It decreases mental stress and tension. When we change our body, in fact, we change our minds.

Colour

Opening up to your own creativity by colouring as well as doodling helps reduce stress and focus mental clarity and can actually calm our amygdala http://blogs.psychcentral.com/emotionally-sensitive/2012/04/self-soothing-calming-the-amgydala/. The focus we put on a project at hand can prevent negative and unhelpful thoughts from entering the mind and help us transition from chaos to calm.

Connect with a Friend or a Group of Friends without Technology!

Face-to-face contact and time presence is what we crave as human beings. Making time to connect on a personal level helps everyone involved live more fully. We see and experience facial expressions and voice tones, etc. that technology just cannot pick up. As well, we get to experience the other person's energy. Be sure to listen, as well as speak and share. Listening offers the opportunity for the other person to simply be heard and attended to. Be sure to turn your phone off, or mute it so that you're not interrupted. There is no substitute for that real-time, in-person connection.

Create Something

The act of creation is an excellent way to be kind to ourselves, for in the process of creating we are expressing our own unique brilliance, and shining our light on a waiting world. For example: you could make some word art, a manifesto, a poem, or you could paint, sketch or draw; do a craft, cook, bake, play music, doodle, write. You might also describe or draw your thoughts and feelings to help you to feel good, positive and happy.

When we choose to create something, rather than "consume" something, we automatically feel a sense of contribution and contentment. We also spark different areas of the brain and provide different pathways to open. Our society is based largely on things: what more can I get, what else can I do? When you let the creative side take over, you allow for new possibilities. So, ignite your inner child and let your creative spirit play.

Do Something You LOVE

Commit to doing something that you love every day. Self-care isn't a special once-a-week thing. It can be an everyday thing. Connecting to the things and the people that you love, and finding joy in individual moments, will leave you feeling refreshed and renewed and more optimistic.

Drink Some Water

Our bodies are made up of up to 60% water according to the Journal of Biological Chemistry. The brain and heart are comprised of about 73% water and our lungs are about 83% water.

When we don't drink enough water, we can often experience symptoms of tiredness, skin issues, increased allergies, increases in inflammation, mental fog, tiredness, lack of ability to focus and decreased levels of physical performance in athletic training as well as weight gain. By consuming adequate water each day, we help our bodies perform and recover to the best of their abilities. Healthy hydration is an intake of water through our foods and beverages throughout the day. Aim to drink some water each hour in the day up to about two litres in total. The key is to not wait until you are feeling thirsty. Furthermore, starting your day with a glass of water, will get you started on the right track! This will help eliminate waste and toxins. Another way of getting increased water every day is by eating raw fruits and veggies. They are dense in water content. You could also monitor your urine: it will be a light yellow colour if you are sufficiently hydrated.

Gratitude Jar for the Self

Write down on slips of coloured paper everything you're grateful for about YOU. Keep this jar close at hand for days when your spirit needs a little lift and a smile. Use a mason jar and decorate it as you see fit. Gratitude moves us into a much calmer energy. It re-balances the nervous system and assists our entire physiology to be more coherent and present.

Journalling: Self-Reflections

Journalling helps evoke a feeling of mindfulness, bringing us into the present moment of reflection. It can help us track how we are feeling and experiencing our world. I found this practice useful in my sport career and it is something I still practice every day. I find it helps me feel more in tune with my goals and my active process for achieving them. I highly recommend the practice.

Massage

Massage helps our body tissues recover from workouts and the daily stress that we place on our bodies and mind.

Meditation and Mindfulness

Spending time each day just with your breath helps train your brain to remain focused in the present moment. We can also use meditation to remind ourselves of positive feelings and moments in our lives, or to project positive intentions forward to future events. Even if you only have one minute to spend in mindfulness meditation, it is better than nothing! So, take those breaths and still your mind, even for a minute!

Nap Time!

The old power nap has many health and mindset benefits. Just taking a 20-minute reset can re-engage your brain and get your body and mind working in sync again. Keep in mind that the more stress we experience, the more important it is to rest and rejuvenate. Athletes know that sleeping helps build new pathways and memories; it enhances learning and encourages faster healing and recovery as well. Be sure to get your zzz's! Below is a sample one-week sleep challenge for you to try out!

Read a Book

Reading helps with our language skills. It helps our mental acuity and focus, as well as our memory. In a time when our world is obsessed with screens and technology, I find it especially important to connect with a book and read the written word. I find it also helps expand my knowledge and stimulate my thinking. And it helps me to relax. I make it a personal practice to read each night before I go to sleep. Start with a small commitment like, 10 minutes, or a chapter. You will surprise yourself with how quickly you can complete a book when you make it a daily practice.

Sing and Dance

Having a kitchen party dance session, or a stereo-blasting bedroom bash, encourages our playful spirit, gets us active and moving, and releases numerous positive feel-good hormones and endorphins. So, when you feel blue, recognize it, download some of your favorite tunes and turn up your music. Let your inner Rockstar shine!

Sound Sleep = Success!

Do you struggle with lack of energy?

Are you working out, eating well and still not reaching your goals?

Sleep quality may be the culprit!

I learned first-hand the critical importance of maintaining a healthy and restful sleep schedule while I was training and racing all over the world. Did you know that lack of sleep contributes to decreased attention and focus, more errors, and a decline in decision-making ability? Luckily, I've never struggled with long-term sleep deprivation. I don't have children. I do own my own company and that can be stressful at times, but I wouldn't consider my life extremely stressful. That being said, I know how it feels to have sleepless nights or a broken sleep. In fact, in the past year, I went through quite a stressful transition period in my life that involved:

- A personal move (twice in the same year, to be exact)
- A re-organization of my business
- A month-long social media campaign and the launch of a new program
- Dealing with the finalization of my divorce in a way that allowed my ex and I to remain friends
- The development and day-to-day running of my company

Stress is the number one contributor to sleep deprivation. Sleep is critically important to our body and minds, and our overall health. During sleep, our hormones go to work to repair damage done by the day-to-day wear and tear on our bodies. Our immune system kicks into gear and our minds sort through thoughts and lessons learned. Lack of sleep hinders our immune system, inhibits memory and cognitive function and can cause alterations in our metabolism.

In short, lack of sleep can turn you into a sugar-craving, grumpy and forgetful version of you. Here are some of the hormones affected by lack of sleep:

Human Growth Hormone (HGH). Our bodies produce this "anti-aging hormone" naturally and we use it to build and repair muscle and other tissue; it breaks down fat and normalizes blood sugar levels, and we secrete it during sleep.

Insulin. Sleep deprivation causes chronically high levels of this hormone. Insulin is vital because it transports blood glucose into our cells to be used as an energy source. High levels lead to weight gain and insulin resistance, which confuses the cells and prevents them from being able to efficiently burn sugar for energy.

Ghrelin. I like to think of this as the hunger gremlin... We feel it when we are hungry, and it signals us to eat. When we are chronically tired, we produce more of this hormone.

How can you build a Strong Sleep Routine to get your ZZZ's?

Here are my seven tips to get you on your way to better sleep tonight:

1. **Follow a Routine!** Our bodies love routine. Try going to bed around the same time each night and rise at the same time each day. I usually start my own bedtime process by 9:00 or 9:15, so that I'm in bed by 9:30 p.m. I typically wake with the sun around 6:30 a.m.

2. **Aim for Eight!** Getting eight hours of bed-time rest and sleep is a sure-fire way to build that strong sleep routine. I always feel best with nine hours of sleep. As I get older and wiser, I sleep more, not less!

3. **Balance your Blood Sugar Before Bed.** Warm apple cider vinegar with water is my go-to elixir for this task. Apple Cider Vinegar (ACV) aids digestion, helps heartburn and stomach upset and balances blood sugar levels, among many other health benefits. ACV also helps with allergy sufferers (like me). When I follow this little health habit, I feel better and have less congestion. Remember that your body needs fast fuel during its wakeful working hours but foods high in calories and sugar will just be wasted at night. Going to bed on a belly full of pasta will spike blood sugar, and ultimately result in more stored fat.

4. **Avoid Screen-Time an Hour Before Bed.** The blue light emitted from electronic devices disturbs our REM sleep, which is that deep sleep that our body and brain needs. This one is incredibly hard for me, as I live alone. But each time I commit to this habit, I feel better

5. **Keep a Journal Near Your Bedside.** If you're anything like me, you sometimes have those "it all comes together" thoughts or "idea sparks" before bed. Jot them down in your journal so you have a container for your thoughts.

6. **Take a Warm Shower Before Bed.** This helps me to rinse off any residue from the day and I simply sleep better with this practice.

7. **Read a Book.** This helps your brain and eyes get into sleep-mode.

Stretching

Stretching helps to decrease injuries, increase flexibility and range of motion as well as improve balance and stability. Stretching also helps us to feel more invigorated with an increase in blood flow. I always found movement, stretching and yoga postures to be a helpful part of my training. Stretching also helps with mental focus and helps us to feel more clear. Even on days when you aren't doing a workout, a stretching session will be of benefit to your body and mindset.

Strong Support System

One of the biggest factors in my success is having a strong support system of people around me.

Look to people in your world who may be part of your support system and honour and nurture those relationships. For me, my support has always come from my family and my closest friends. I also have reached out to my coaches and some work colleagues as mentors. Remember that you get to choose who you surround yourself with. Your environment can serve you in the most supportive way.

Take it Outside!

Being outside helps build up our endorphins and feel-good energy. Daylight and natural energy from the sun help us to absorb Vitamin D, a powerful hormone responsible for many physiological reactions in our bodies. Nature has a natural calming effect on the nervous system. When we connect with the Earth, and breathe in fresh air, we are rebalanced, and we absorb negative ions, which helps our mental health.

You may have experienced the effects of negative ions when you last visited a beach, a waterfall, or a forest. We get a sense of euphoria and alertness that is much different from how we feel when we are inside. Next time you're in need of a natural mood boost, head outside and absorb some negative ions!

Talk to a Friend

Instead of connecting on social media, what about popping by for a visit, or dialing your friend's phone number to talk voice-to-voice! Immerse yourself in the moment and truly appreciate your time with them. Listen to how you feel while hearing their voice, and notice your energy as you connect with them.

Time-Out from Social Media and Multi-Media Consumption

This seems like a small thing, but small pains lead to big time gains! The act of removing distractions is incredibly helpful when the goal is to intensely focus or perform at your best. I used this strategy as an athlete and forgot about its importance in my business life until I re-introduced it. I am fairly extreme with it. I do let people closest to me know how to reach me. But I turn off all news and social media for the entire day leading up to a big event, and only choose to open email during scheduled times. Even television and Netflix go off. I turn to restorative practices as mentioned above and spend time mostly journalling, reading, listening to music, etc. You will be surprised at how much more energy and clear focus it will give you. Try it!

ABOUT the Author

Karen Furneaux is a three-time Olympian and two-time World Champion in the sport of sprint kayaking. She has won nine medals at the world championships, including two gold over her 20-year athletic career, and she was a member of CBC's Olympic Broadcast Team in Rio in the summer of 2016. Through her company, I Promise Performance Inc., Karen speaks with international audiences about the connection between health, mindset and performance. She holds a Master of Science Degree in Kinesiology from Dalhousie University with a specialization in Sport Psychology, as well as numerous sport and personal development training certifications. Karen has undergone extensive Team and Leadership training through Cornell University and she is a licensed HeartMath provider.

Karen has recently been inducted into the Nova Scotia Sport Hall of Fame and she has been named one of the top 15 most successful athletes in Nova Scotia sport history. Her training and experience allow her to support her clients as they build resilience and manage stress, and she is passionate about engaging and empowering youth, volunteering her time to the Nova Scotia Sport Hall of Fame - Education Program. Karen has created a mentorship and empowerment group for girls aged 12-18 called "Strong Beauty." It helps young girls become more self-confident, develop a strong, positive body image, develop and practice healthy lifestyle habits and successfully manage times of transition.

ACKNOWLEDGEMENTS

I'd like to acknowledge the team of people who helped bring this book into the world. My editor, Susan Crossman, your passion for writing and your commitment to doing authentic work resonated with me from our first conversation. Thank you for your detailed eye and your suggestions as to how to make this work stronger. My design editor and branding consultant, Janet Rouss, thank you for your persistence and for believing in me and this book. Thank you for continuously checking in on me to see if I'm OK and for your innovative ideas to move this book further into the world. Thank you for helping me shepherd this book through the self-publishing process.

To my Accelerated Learning Pods (ALPS) write-your-book mastermind team at the Canadian Association of Professional Speakers (CAPS), thank you for your knowledge and experience and willingness to share and, above all, for your support.

Thank you to my Advanced Management and Mentoring Program (AMMP) mastermind group at The Centre for Women in Business. Thank you for your wise and thoughtful council and well as your friendship.

Thank you to all the fearless and courageous women entrepreneurs out there in the world, your spirit and combined energy helped me to complete this book. I truly feel the vortex of strong beauty energy when I sit to write and I'm grateful to be part of the community.

I'd also like to thank my ski trip and travel buddy, Louise White for her proofreading skills and generosity as well as her fun spirit on the slopes!

Finally, thank you to my friends and family for asking me how the book is coming along, cheering me on along the journey and keeping me accountable and on track! Thank you for your unwavering love, belief and support.

I am forever grateful to all of you.